Linda Blain and the braves, along with the strength imparted by faith in God when the senseless greed of war foists tests even on young children. Written so that children can identify with young Halinka, *Enduring the Empire* will draw in reader of all ages.

—Ruth Smith Meyer
Author of *Not Easily Broken*, *Not Far from the Tree* and *Tyson's Sad Bad Day*

What Young Readers Are Saying:

Your book was one of the best books I've ever heard! It was very, very detailed, and you felt like you were in the book.

—Paige

I loved the twists and turns in this story. Some of the parts in this story really catch you, especially when I was really holding my breath! (I turned purple.) My favourite part was everything! I think this is an important story to tell, because it makes you realize that we are so lucky to have a safe country and shelter.

—Karis

I loved your fascinating story. I loved how you thought to tell the whole world about this great story. You wrote it so people can tell how thankful we are.

—Caitlyn

All the parts jump out at you. It's important because it's mostly real. Every time, you just wanted to keep going.

—Taryn

I loved the book, and because it was mostly real, it made it even cooler. I couldn't even pick out a favourite part because I thought it was all so great! I really think there should be a sequel, and I can't wait to hear it.

—Lauren

I loved the book, especially the way each chapter left you with a cliff-hanger. I think this story is important to tell because it is reality. It shows what could happen to us.

—Keegan

I think the book really got you attached to it because if one person was taken away it would have been harder to survive. This story is important to tell because lots of people died and those people might be forgotten. You don't want that to happen.

—Bailey

Enduring the EMPIRE

LINDA BLAIN

ENDURING THE EMPIRE
Copyright © 2020 by Linda Blain

Author photo taken by Paula Tizzard of Paula Tizzard Photography. paulatizzard.com.

All rights reserved. Neither this publication nor any part of this publication may be reproduced or transmitted in any form or by any means, electronic or mechanical, including photocopying, recording or any information storage and retrieval system, without permission in writing from the author.

This is a work of historical fiction. The dialogue has been fictionalized, but the story is based on the family account of the author. Any references to historical events, real people, or real places are used fictitiously. Other names, characters, places and events are products of the authors imagination, and any resemblance to actual events, places or persons, living or dead, is entirely coincidental.

Scripture quotations are taken from the New King James Version®. Copyright © 1982 by Thomas Nelson, Inc. Used by permission. All rights reserved.

Printed in Canada

Print ISBN: 978-1-4866-1306-9
ebook ISBN: 978-1-4866-1307-6

Word Alive Press
119 De Baets Street, Winnipeg, MB R2J 3R9
www.wordalivepress.ca

Cataloguing in Publication may be obtained through Library and Archives Canada

CONTENTS

	Acknowledgements	vii

BOOK ONE: STOLEN FREEDOM

	Prologue	3
1.	Unrest Brewing	5
2.	The Secret Room	13
3.	Surprise Visitors	20
4.	A Day Out	26
5.	The Store	37
6.	A New School Day	47
7.	Wartime Christmas	56
8.	Disappearances	60
9.	The Black List	68
10.	A Time to Say Goodbye	78

BOOK TWO: WELCOME TO THE THIRD REICH

	Prologue	85
11.	The Train Ride	89
12.	The New Border	95
13.	First Camp	99
14.	A Close Call	105
15.	The Song	114
16.	The Bugs	117
17.	The Shower	120
18.	Pabianice	126

19.	Summoned	132
20.	The Search	138
21.	The Outhouse	142
22.	All for the Fatherland	145

BOOK THREE: INSIDE GERMANY

	Prologue	151
23.	Unexpected News	153
24.	Tata's Return	161
25.	A New School	168
26.	Hitler Youth/League of German Girls	173
27.	Allies Become Enemies	177
28.	Good News for Jean	181
29.	Turning Point	186
30.	A Secret Told	190
31.	Struggling to Escape Hunger	196
32.	Taken	200
33.	Bombs	204
34.	Too Close!	208
35.	Northeim	211
36.	Surrender!	215
37.	Freedom!	222

What Happened To	229
Author's Note	231

ACKNOWLEDGEMENTS

A special thanks to:

My mom, without whom I couldn't have done this and who patiently answered my seemingly perpetual list of questions.

My dad, who loved his family dearly but struggled with PTSD all of his life because of his own World War II experiences.

Aunt Jean and Aunt Anne for filling in some of the gaps about your lives in Wolkowysk, Poland and Germany.

Authors Gweneth Wilmsmith, Ruth Smith-Meyer, and Barbara Greenwood for their professional critiquing and invaluable advice.

Donna Bennett, who read my first draft and liked it: You made my day.

Wanda Zynomirski, Randy Martin, Rob Poirier, Erica Huff, Kim King, Charity Hodgins, Janet Prout, Marg Brain and the wonderful staff at Oxbow Public School for taking the time to read or listen to the manuscript and for giving your words of encouragement.

My husband, John, my four adult children—Derek, Matthew, Justin, Selena—my daughter-in-law, Laura, and my two grandchildren for letting me ramble on and for being such awesome sounding boards. You are so precious in my heart.

A special thank you to Tia Friesen, Kerry Wilson, and the staff at Word Alive Press for your enthusiasm and amazing editing skills. I couldn't have done it without your expertise!

It is my hope that each reader will come away with a greater appreciation and understanding of what so many endured during World War II — "Lest we forget!"

Book One
STOLEN FREEDOM

"Where do wars and fights come from among you? Do they not come from your desires for pleasure that war in your members? You lust and do not have. You murder and covet and cannot obtain."

—James 4:1–2

PROLOGUE

The warm, golden sun had already sunk below the crest of the surrounding hills, casting long, dark shadows over the small city of Wolkowysk (pronounced "Volkovisk") in Eastern Poland.

Two legends had been associated with the name Wolkowysk for hundreds of years. The first was called the Stone Legend. It was believed that the area at one time was an ancient forest filled with many impassable bogs. Two robbers, Volek and Vysek, made it a dangerous place. Their violent ways deterred people from passing through or even entering at all. Eventually, the ruling Prince Zabeyko rallied his followers to hunt them down and kill them. He engraved a large stone on their gravesite, and the city's name supposedly came from this stone. First it was called Volekovysek (meaning *Volek* and *Vysek*), and then later it was changed to Volkovysk. Today there is an archaeological site of the Stone Legend called Muravelnic.

The second legend associated with its name was called the *volkolaks* legend. A *volkolak* was a man who had supposedly sold his heart to the devil and eventually died in mortal sin. He was then transformed into a wolf. It was believed many *volkolaks* ran through the fields and forests howling and hunting for food. *Volk* is translated "wolf" in English, and *Vysk* means "howl" in modern Russian. Hence, the name means "wolf-howl."

Chapter One
UNREST BREWING

Throughout the city on the night of September 11, 1939, many children were settling in for a good night's sleep. Ten-year-old Halinka snuggled down deep into her grandmother's handmade feather comforter as her mother gently tucked her in. She noticed that the creases of concern on Mama's face made her appear older than her thirty-six years. A wave of fear caused Halinka's stomach to tighten uncomfortably.

"Will everything be all right, Mama?" she whispered.

"Yes," said Mama, stroking Halinka's hair. "Everything will be fine. God is with us. You must get some sleep now." After a parting kiss on the cheek, she doused the light and left the room.

Under Hitler's rule, Germany had already invaded their country. Ten days earlier, the German military had roared across the Polish countryside like a raging storm. After advancing over three hundred kilometres with little resistance, they viciously assaulted the capital city of Warsaw, which was now fighting for its very life.

Although numbering over one million men, the Polish army was not ready for the type of combat taking place. Their equipment dated back to World War I, and they were fewer in number than their advancing enemies. Many still rode on horseback.[1]

Because of the German invasion, most of the Polish army was on the country's western border. Rumours abounded that Russia would invade Poland from the east. Many of their Ukrainian comrades across the southern border were receiving propaganda pamphlets from Russia, encouraging them to turn on their Polish neighbours. Fear spread throughout Poland like ripples across a windswept pond.

Terrifying thoughts of war disturbed Halinka's sleep. Tossing and turning, she imagined soldiers coming to take her family away or killing them all. Eventually, her mother's soothing words came to her

---

[1] Germany had developed a new style of warfare called *blitzkrieg*, or "lightning strike." First, they would send in a massive air attack and heavily bomb a region. Then, when the bombing ended, a huge army would rush in and take over.

mind. She forced herself to think about them and finally fell asleep.

Halinka awoke early the next morning with all thoughts of war far away, as though lost in a dream. After stretching and yawning, she bounded out of bed and scurried to her older sister's bedside.

"Wake up," she whispered to Therese, gently nudging her. Before Therese could respond, Halinka sprinted out of the bedroom, down the hall, out the back door, and across the lawn to the outhouse.

I'll beat her this time, she thought as the morning wind blew her sandy blonde hair into long, flowing streamers. The girls usually made a game of who would be the first to awaken and get ready for the day.

Minutes later she ran back inside the house to take a sponge bath and was delighted to see there was no sign of her sister. She went into the utility room to get ready. It was a multi-purpose room that was also used for laundry and storage. Shelves on each wall held cans and jars of food. Every evening the girls would bring their clothes and hang them up, ready to wear to school the next day. In the rear was the entrance to an underground root cellar. Next to that, a small private area was partitioned off with wooden slats for the bathtub. A small well outside the house was connected by an underground pipe to the utility room, which had a manual pump. This was the new way to bring water into homes. No more drawing it out of a well with ropes and pails and carrying it inside. Water could now be pumped into the house at any time of the year, even in winter. Each evening Tata[2] stoked the kitchen fire so there would be hot water available for the next morning.

Halinka reached for her wash bowl and placed it on a wooden table. She carefully poured in a pitcher of cold water and then added a ladle of hot water from the kitchen stove to warm it up. She splashed the water over her face and soaped her hands and arms to the elbow and rinsed them quickly. After drying herself, Halinka hung her towel on one of the large wooden pegs mounted on the wall.

Turning around, she grasped the porcelain knob of the door and pulled it open. She gasped with surprise! There stood Therese.

"That was close," exclaimed Therese. "I was hoping to beat you, but you won fair and square—again!" They both laughed.

"Maybe next time you'll win," Halinka remarked as she hurried off to get her school books.

---

2 Pronounced "Ta ta," which means "Dad."

A short while later, the Kutsza family, all except Halinka, sat at the huge wooden kitchen table handmade years earlier by her grandfather. Jean, the oldest at fifteen, sat on one side of Tata. Beside her was thirteen-year-old Anne. Next came twelve-year-old Therese and, close to Mama, two-year-old Helen. Last of all, propped up in a pillow-filled chair between Mama and Tata, sat six-month-old baby Paul.

"Good morning, everyone!" shouted Halinka as she ran into the room and took her seat. "Sorry for being late." A few chuckles could be heard around the table. This was not unusual. Tata cleared his throat to get everyone's attention and looked directly at her. He sighed, knowing it was no use reprimanding her for being late.

Their live-in nanny, Nina, stood behind Tata with a large platter in her hands, ready to serve another tasty breakfast. She had been with them for the past three years and was just like another member of the family. She often took the children for picnics and walks in the countryside. Her friendly manner and genuine kindness were what attracted them to her. She often picked flowers from the garden to brighten Mama's kitchen, showing her thoughtfulness and care for the family.

"Are you ready for food?" Nina smiled.

"Yes!" was the chorus from everyone. She handed the plate to Tata, who then led in a short prayer of thanksgiving for the meal.

Breakfast was fun at the Kutsza house, mostly because of the ice cream. Since they owned a grocery store-delicatessen, Mama prepared lots of food to sell. This included homemade ice cream made from her personal secret recipe. Every evening she would mix and cook a batch, letting it sit overnight. A delivery man on a horse-drawn wagon would bring ice early each morning. The ice, which was harvested from ponds and lakes, was placed in a large barrel containing a smaller one filled with the mixed ingredients. While it cooled, Jean and Anne would take turns cranking the handle that beat the mixture. Before long, it became thick, mouth-watering ice cream. After breakfast, the children were given the leftovers from the barrel and beaters. They always looked forward to this tasty treat.[3]

"How's the ice cream this morning?" inquired Halinka, to no one in particular. Eating it was a highlight of her day.

"Great," responded Anne. "Thank goodness Jean did most of the cranking. It seemed somewhat stiffer today."

---

[3] The ice harvested in winter was kept in "ice houses" and packed with straw or sawdust for insulation. This way it was available over the summer and would often stay frozen until the following winter.

"You did your share of the work too, Anne," encouraged Jean.

"Thanks. I guess it is easier with two people sharing the work."

As Nina and Mama passed the bacon and eggs around the table, Halinka glanced sideways to see Rex, their faithful German shepherd, sitting nearby, his eyes fixed on the plate of food. *Good boy; you'll get yours soon.*

"Here, Halinka," said Anne, passing the plate.

"Thank you," she replied, placing some food on her plate before handing it to Therese.

Chewing slowly, Halinka carefully looked around the room. *Good! No one is watching.* She guided her fork full of bacon toward her mouth and then changed its direction and tossed it under the table. At that same moment, Therese winked mischievously at her and did the same. Rex slowly got up and sauntered under the table, where he quickly gulped down his treats.

The girls loved this morning ritual of feeding him. They knew he enjoyed it as much as they did. Looking at each other they began to giggle, thinking they had fooled everyone again.

Nina suddenly leaned between them. "Girls," she whispered, "do not be so wasteful. Someday you may wish you had that bacon."

Halinka had such a strong distaste for bacon that she felt no guilt over the dog eating her portion. There was always plenty to eat in their home. As far as she was concerned, there would always be enough. Fruit from the orchard was cooked and preserved in jars. Mama did the same with pork and fowl. Dried sausage hung in clusters from the large ceiling beams in the kitchen. Potatoes were placed in the root cellar. Beans and carrots were purchased from the gardener who had his plot behind a hill known by the townspeople as "Swedish Mountain."

Rex needs to stay strong and healthy, she reasoned. However, with war raging not far away and Nina's foreboding words, an uneasiness settled upon both of the girls. Sheepishly, they looked away.

Today they still had lots of food—including ice cream—so all seemed well. They had no idea how true Nina's words would become.

Chapter Two
THE SECRET ROOM

Mama and Tata huddled close to their shortwave radio, straining to hear news of the war.[4]

"Poland is desperately fighting for its very existence against invading Germany," announced the broadcaster. "Warsaw (Poland's capital city) has almost fallen. It appears that absolute defeat is only days away. Where, we must ask, are Poland's allies?"[5]

---

4 A shortwave transmitter is one that can transmit radio programs to almost anywhere on earth and operates at the high end of the radio wave spectrum. During World War II, shortwave radio was an inexpensive way to hear news and other programs from all over the free world. It was very common for people in countries taken over by Germany, for example, to listen to stations from Britain. This way they would get accurate news and not just lies and propaganda.

5 Britain and France did declare war but neglected to act. France began a military offensive but when met with resistance stopped short and never again regained momentum. England bluffed that they would attack with the hope that Germany would back down. They were wrong.

Such news changed the daily routines of the townspeople. On this particular morning, Halinka's parents did not come for breakfast, nor was any ice cream made.

"Hurry up," called an anxious Therese, "or we'll be late for school."

"I'm coming," answered Halinka, tossing her leather satchel over her shoulder.

"Wait," ordered Tata, coming up from the root cellar. "Today there will be no school."

"Why not?" asked the girls. They were surprised by this announcement. Tata never let them miss school unless they were sick.

"Today we must work together and move food into our secret room. Wait here while I get your sisters."

The girls' sense of joy quickly disappeared.

One year earlier, when Tata had constructed their new home, he had built a hidden room. It was to be used for hiding food and emergency supplies. Memories of the near starvation that he and his family had experienced during the First World War motivated him to take extra precautions in case of another.

"Do you know anything about a secret room?" asked Therese with a puzzled look.

"Yes, I do," Halinka said. She thought back to a few weeks earlier, when Mama had been ill ...

The Secret Room

"Halinka," called Mama from her sick bed.

"Yes, Mama?"

"I'm not feeling well today, and I need you to do something important for me."

"Sure."

"Nina needs some flour to bake fresh bread for the store. If you help me up, I can show you what to do."

Halinka took Mama's hand. Slowly they walked to the utility room.

"Here, Halinka, help me with this ladder."

Together they carried it to within a few metres of the entrance door. Looking up, Halinka saw the many narrow wooden slats that formed an attractive crisscross pattern on the ceiling. Unknown to her, Tata had designed it this way to conceal a secret opening.

"Do you see that section above the ladder?" asked Mama, pointing upward.

"Yes."

"Climb up and lift it to one side. Behind it is the attic. Once you get inside you must find the chimney. Behind it is a trap door leading down into our secret room. There will be a hook for hanging the lamp."

Halinka was filled with excitement. After climbing up the ladder and sliding a section of the ceiling aside, she found herself looking into a dark opening. Mama then reached up and handed her the coal oil lamp.

"Be careful. Make sure you step only on the wooden ceiling supports."

"Okay, Mama."

Holding the lamp up, she slowly made her way through the opening. The burning wick softly illuminated her immediate surroundings. There was only a small space in which to crawl; stepping on the wrong spot could mean falling through the ceiling and crashing to the floor below. Worse yet, should the lamp tip over or break, a fire was sure to happen. With a tight grip on the lamp's handle, she held it up in search of the chimney.

Her gaze fell to the attic floor. It was covered with dry hay, which was used for insulation and would burn very quickly if set on fire. If such a thing happened, there would be no escape.

Where is it? Halinka wondered. Mama told her it would be off on an angle to her right about ten paces. As she stretched the lamp as far as possible away from her body, the dark grey stones of the chimney suddenly appeared out of the darkness.

Brushing away the hay to make a narrow path, she inched her way to the rear of the chimney. There she found the small trap door—the entrance to the secret room.

"There it is," she gasped. "I found it, Mama."

Her hands trembled with excitement. She pulled on a round steel handle and it creaked open.

The Secret Room

A ladder descended down into the darkness. After hanging the lamp on the hook Mama had referred to, she lowered herself through the opening.

The room was very narrow, slightly wider than a regular doorway, and lined with thin shelves, most of which were empty. At the end was a white linen bag of flour. Beside it was a small tin pail.

Using the scoop that was in the flour bag, she filled the pail. After tightly resealing the bag, she took the pail and slowly made her way along the narrow room and back up the ladder. When she reached the top, she placed the pail off to one side, grabbed the lantern, and climbed out. She then closed the trap door and spread hay around to conceal it. Very carefully, while holding both the lantern and the flour, she crawled back to the opening where Mama waited.

"Great job, Halinka," Mama said with relief in her voice. "Here, let me take those."

Halinka passed her the flour and lantern, returned to spread some hay over the path she had made crawling, and came down the ladder.

"Oh, that was so exciting," said Halinka.

"Wow," exclaimed Therese, "I didn't even know we had such a room."

Before Halinka could respond, Tata's booming voice interrupted them.

"Halinka, Therese, come with me! You're needed in the root cellar to pass up food to Mama."

Later, with Tata directing everyone, they formed a human chain to move the food to the secret room. As much as possible was to be stored for the future.

"Why do we have to put all this in the secret room?" whispered Halinka as she passed Therese a jar of preserved meat.

"I don't know," answered Therese. "Why don't you ask Tata?"

"I will, but not right now. He's too busy."

Most of the morning was spent working hard. Finally, Halinka had an opportunity to ask Tata.

"We may be getting surprise visitors," he responded grimly.

She was afraid to ask what he meant. *Why is everything changing so quickly? Our food surely won't run out—will it? We have always had so much of everything.*

After the storage room was filled, the family gathered for a quick lunch. Later, the store shelving was dismantled and the storefront sign taken down. All of it was broken up and burned in the fireplace. Tata wanted to leave no evidence that they had any extra food hidden in their home. A single bed and dresser were placed in the empty room. It now looked like an ordinary bedroom.

That evening after supper, they all fell exhausted into their beds. Halinka quietly said her evening prayers and thought about the day's unusual activities. She was drifting gently into sleep when Therese's voice suddenly cut through the silent darkness.

"Halinka, are you awake?"

"I am now."

"Why do you suppose we moved all the food into the secret room? What did Tata say?"

"I don't really know, and all Tata would say is that we may be getting some unexpected visitors. They must want to take our food."

"They can't be very nice people!" exclaimed Therese. "I don't think I'll like them very much."

"Me neither."

Slowly slipping into a deep slumber, Halinka could hear a low rumbling sound off in the distance. It sounded like thunder, but a part of her suspected it was from another, more dangerous, source.

Chapter Three
SURPRISE VISITORS

"Hurry up, Halinka. Get up!" shouted Therese, shaking her awake. "Come and see what's happening."

"What's going on?" Halinka asked, rubbing her eyes and sitting up. From outside came the sound of many loud engines.

"Have a look," answered Therese, pointing out the window.

At that moment, little Helen raced into the room. She jumped up on the bed and hung on to Halinka. The noisy commotion had scared her.

"Now, now, it's going to be all right." Halinka gave her a hug. "Come to the window with Therese and me."

Peering out the window, they saw that the street was filled with large grey tanks, military vehicles, and soldiers, who filed steadily past their home.

"Let's go outside for a better look," suggested Halinka. She took Helen by the hand.

When they reached the kitchen, they found everyone else looking out the window. Helen ran over to Mama.

"Come on, Halinka," whispered Therese, "follow me."

Unnoticed, they slipped out the front door onto the small landing. The noise of the heavy machinery was almost overwhelming. It made them shiver to see the huge grey battle tanks, armed with massive guns, rumble past. Trucks filled with men and supplies, and line after line of armed marching soldiers, went by.

Halinka wrapped her arms around Therese, trembling with fright. Tears welled up in their eyes as they realized what was happening ... Russia was invading their country.

They slowly stepped back into the house, closed the door, and ran into the kitchen. Their minds were suddenly filled with a hundred questions.

"Mama—" but before Halinka could finish, gunshots and horrible screams came from outside.

Tata turned away from the window, drawing the curtains closed, looking tired and worn. He knew only too well the hardships a war can bring. His past experiences of living through the First World War seemed like only yesterday.

"We must be brave," he said solemnly to everyone. "Remember, no matter how dark the darkness, light always overcomes. Even a small candle in a large, dark room will make a difference." He paused to let it sink in and then continued, "We have each other, but more importantly, we have our faith. We must stay strong in God. He will see us through whatever comes."

Mama nodded. "No one is to leave the house. Everyone will stay inside until Tata and I believe it is safe. Is this clear?"

"Yes, Mama," agreed everyone.

"Where's Nina?" asked Jean, suddenly aware of her absence.

"She hasn't arrived," replied Mama, "but she should be safe. She's with her parents in the country."

It was Nina's weekend off work. Usually she would go to visit her parents every other Friday and return on the Sunday evening.

"Wait a minute," said Tata, seeing a look of alarm in everyone's eyes. "It's important to not let fear overcome us. We must stay busy doing our chores to keep our minds occupied."

A few days later, around noon, while Halinka was sweeping the floor, a loud knock was heard at the front door. Before anyone could answer, it burst open and two armed soldiers entered. Halinka was wide-eyed with fright. *Will they shoot us? Have they come to take us away?*

Surprise Visitors

A movement out of the corner of her eye made her turn and look. Tata walked calmly into the room and stood in front of her, facing the soldiers.

"What can we do for you?" he asked quietly in Russian. He did not want the intruders to feel threatened and act violently.

The soldiers spoke to each other for a few moments and then ordered everyone to stay where they were. One remained by the door while the other began searching the house.

Mama, who was holding baby Paul, looked intensely at Halinka and cleared her throat.

Halinka looked at her mother. *Why is Mama looking at me that way?* As Mama's gaze moved away from her to the hallway, it became apparent. Helen was alone in her bed sleeping. Should she wake up frightened, it might cause the soldiers to become alarmed and act in a hostile manner. Slowly leaning the broom she was holding against the wall, she began nonchalantly walking down the hallway. At the doorway to little Helen's bedroom, the sound of loud footsteps coming from behind made her freeze. A strong urge to run almost overcame her, but what was the point? Where could she go? What good would it do?

The searching soldier walked toward her. As he passed by, he gave her a cold, hard stare. Halinka turned away. She did not want to encourage his attention. He began looking into each room and then entered through Helen's door. Halinka prayed for her sister's protection. The soldier exited a few moments later and went back to his partner.

As he disappeared around a corner of the hallway, Halinka slipped into Helen's room. Relief swept over her as she saw that Helen lay undisturbed and sound asleep on her bed. *Good. She doesn't even know he was here.* Satisfied, she quickly made her way back to the others.

The soldiers had just departed, and Mama and Tata were engaged in a serious conversation. They looked at her, and she nodded in a way that said "All is well."

"It's a good thing the store looks like a bedroom!" exclaimed Tata.

"Yes," agreed Mama. "Hopefully they won't come back to search for food or other supplies."

Day after day the Russians busied themselves by looting homes, stores, and businesses, even extending themselves many kilometres into the surrounding countryside. They took as much as they could of food and anything they deemed valuable. Every store in town was emptied. Trucks were filled with what the people had worked so hard to attain and then driven away to Russia. No one dared resist, as it would mean certain death.

Businesses, schools, and churches were closed. The people were left desolate, and most were now unemployed. Many fled west, away from the Russian occupation and into the hands of the Germans, where they believed it would be safer. Everyone felt displaced.

What do we do next? Tata wondered, but a plan was taking shape in his mind.

There had been little resistance when Russia invaded Poland. Most of Poland's military was already fighting the German advance in the west. Only a small army remained to protect the eastern border.

Over the radio came the sad news: "Warsaw has surrendered." Germany now occupied the western half of Poland, and Russia staked its claim in the east. A feeling of hopelessness and deep despair prevailed among the Polish people. Like dark clouds ushering in a storm, the invaders' presence brought a sense of impending doom.

Tata refused to allow the country's defeat to rob him of hope. Gazing at his family, he determined that with God's help, they would survive.

Chapter Four
A DAY OUT

By the middle of October, most of the invading military had moved on to complete their conquest of Polish territory and put down any pockets of resistance. Some soldiers remained in Wolkowysk as an occupying force. It was a known fact that Stalin and Hitler were working together to divide the country. The eastern half would be owned by Russia and the western half by Germany.[6]

About this time, people began venturing out from their homes. Mama and Tata visited with nearby neighbours and spoke with them concerning the present troubling times. They all wondered about the future. How long would this war last?

Late one morning, Halinka and Therese were leaning over the sofa, looking out the window. How

---

6   The Russian invasion lasted only twenty days, at the end of which the country was divided up between Germany and Russia. The non-aggression pact they signed was intended to last for ten years with an automatic five-year extension.

they yearned to be outdoors again; it had been almost a month since they had been out.

"Therese," whispered Halinka, "let's ask Tata if we can go outside."

"You ask. You're a lot bolder than I am."

With a serious and determined look, Halinka strode up to her parents, who were sitting in the kitchen.

"Mama, Tata, can Therese and I go outside? Most of the army is gone, and lots of people are walking around. We'll be careful and promise to stay away from any soldiers. Please?" she pleaded.

"I don't know," replied Tata. "It's still very dangerous."

"What about Pan (pronounced "pun") and Pani (pronounced "Punee") Kowalski? Remember, Mama? You were wondering how they're getting along. Therese and I could go see them."

"Well," said Mama thoughtfully, "I did want to bring them some food. The stores have been closed for so long, and I'm sure they will be running out by now. I worry about them going hungry."

"Oh, Mama," exclaimed Halinka, her voice escalating with excitement, "just let us go, please!"

Mama looked at Tata. "Ludwig, what shall we do?"

"Well, they are only children," he said, and then he paused in thought. "The soldiers will not be threatened by them, and it would be good to see how our friends are doing and to give them some food. Would you be all right if they go?"

Mama slowly nodded her approval.

"All right, Halinka," Tata conceded, "but only under certain conditions."

"Thank you! Thank you! Yes, whatever you say." She gave a huge grin.

Therese heaved a sigh of relief. Quietly standing around the corner, she had heard every word. *Leave it to Halinka to make a way.* At last they could leave the house. It had been so difficult staying indoors. Even playing their favourite card games of Pig and Outhouse was getting boring. They felt like kittens being held in a cage much too small for their size.

"You must not venture off on your own. Stay together and, whenever possible, close to other people. Avoid any soldiers, and be back within an hour," Tata ordered.

"We promise we will, Tata."

Within minutes the girls were helping Mama fill a small, cotton sack with food. "Be especially careful with the glass jars," she instructed, handing the small yet heavy sack to Therese.

Brimming with excitement, they put on their coats, hugged and kissed their parents, and headed for the door. Opening it slowly, they peered out. All was clear. Not a soldier was in sight, so they quietly departed.

A Day Out

Tata and Pan Kowalski had been good friends for many years. They'd worked together in the local police force when Tata was an assistant to the chief. Once, while apprehending thieves, Tata was shot in the leg. Even after many operations it did not heal properly. Later, he trained Pan to take over his position and then took an early retirement.

Pani, Pan's wife, always welcomed the Kutsza family when they visited. Halinka loved the way Pani kept her home so nicely decorated, especially the fancy, white curtains that hung in the windows. They reminded her of delicate snowflakes fastened together.

Halinka was jolted out of her daydream by the sound of her sister's voice. "Halinka, look at that!"

The cobblestones in front of them were damaged and overturned in many places. Wide jagged ruts along the surface reminded her of furrows in a freshly plowed field.

"The holes and gouges are from the tanks," said Therese sadly. "They're so heavy, they've chewed up our beautiful streets, and look over there at the park."

The girls stopped in their tracks, stunned by the sight. Small trees were knocked over, lawns dug up like the streets, and flower gardens destroyed. It did not resemble the colourful and happy place they once knew.

"Come on, Therese, let's go. We've only got so much time."

Soon they rounded the familiar street corner to Pan and Pani's house. So far, no soldiers or vehicles had been seen. Neither were many people out and about. Nervously they made their way to the front door and knocked.

Pani's worried face suddenly appeared through the curtains on their right. Realizing who they were, her expression immediately changed to that of joy. The door flung open, and a smiling Pani beckoned them to enter.

"Come in, come in, girls. Oh my, how good it is to see you!" She wrapped them in her arms. "Are you alone? How is the family?"

"There are just the two of us," replied Therese. "Everyone else is fine and at home."

"Where are Pan and Irka (pronounced "Ee-rka")?" asked Halinka, referring to Pani's husband and daughter.

"Pan is out getting firewood. Irka has gone to my parents' home in the country. Because of Pan's position on the police force, we may be drawing some unwanted attention from the Russians. We believe it is safer for her there." The hurt was evident in her expression and voice, clearly showing how much she missed her daughter.

"There now, what is this?" she asked, changing the subject. "You brought us something?"

A Day Out

"Yes," Therese nodded, "Mama and Tata want you to have this food." She held up the cotton bag.

"Bless you," said Pani with tears in her eyes, "we've just about run out. You and your family are so kind. Let's see what you've brought, and then we will have some of my favourite tea."

The visit was short and wonderful, and all too quickly it was time to leave. The girls promised Pani they would pass on her news to their parents. After leaving, they waved one final time before turning the street corner.

As they started down the next street they came to an abrupt halt. Two Russian soldiers were walking toward them. No one else was in sight. A feeling of dread crept over the girls. In moments, it became panic.

"Run," yelled Halinka.

As one, they spun around and took off. From behind they heard a gruff "Stop!" but the girls had no intention of stopping. Fear gripped their hearts. The soldiers' heavy footsteps followed as they took up the chase. Twisting and turning through small alleyways, the girls tried to lose them. They could not! Their pursuers were slowly gaining.

"Keep running, Halinka," cried Therese. Being taller and of a slighter build than Halinka, she was always the faster runner. Halinka pushed herself harder than ever. *They can't catch us! They can't catch us!* The words swirled around in her mind.

As they wound their way through some yards and gardens, Halinka spotted a small hedge.

"Look, over there. Hurry, let's hide." Her foot hit a wooden basket as she rounded the side of the hedge. Kicking it out of the way, the girls crouched out of sight. Halinka glanced down and was amazed to see a small trap door. "Help me," she cried. Together they pulled it open. Narrow steps descended down into darkness.

"Let's go," urged Therese. Halinka hurried down the steps with Therese right behind. Just before closing the door, she pulled the basket toward her. She was hoping to use it for cover. Fortunately, the basket stopped rolling and came to rest on top of the trap door.

Down in their hideout, they were enveloped in a thick blackness. The cold and dampness made them shiver, so they huddled together.

"I hope we've lost them," whispered Halinka.

"Yes. If they find us here, we're finished."

At that moment from above came the sound of angry voices drawing near.

Oh no, thought Halinka, *if they open the door, we are caught.* With the soldiers now directly above them, Halinka's breathing became heavier with fright, so she forced herself to breathe quietly. The girls held each other tightly, silently hoping and praying they wouldn't be found.

The voices slowly began to fade away. Halinka sighed with relief. The soldiers were going away. "Should we go now?"

"Not yet," cautioned Therese, "it may be a trap. They may be waiting for us."

Halinka's imagination couldn't help but run wild in the damp darkness. *What if a rat or other animal is down here with us? What if a snake is slithering near us right now? Well*, she reasoned, *that's still better than a soldier.*

"Okay, let's go," Therese announced with a hushed voice, much to Halinka's relief.

From somewhere out of the darkness came a small whimper. "What's that?" Halinka gasped, getting ready to bolt up the ladder.

"Please," it was a little quivering voice, "I won't hurt you."

"Is that you, Irka?" asked Therese. "You sound like Irka."

"Yes, it's me, and I'm alone."

"How did you get here?" asked a bewildered Halinka. "Your mother told us you were sent away to a safe place out in the country."

"It's a long story," sobbed Irka. "Can you take me home with you now? I'll tell you about it later."

"Yes," said Therese, "you must be freezing. Come on with us. Tata will know what to do."

After carefully climbing up the ladder, Therese slowly lifted the trap door and peered out. All was clear. Once outside, the girls got their first look at Irka's haggard appearance. Dirt was smeared on her face and clothing. Her hair was matted and messy. Without a word, they fell into each other's arms and began to cry. It was all so crazy how everything had changed.

"Come on, we've got to hurry," urged Therese. "Mama and Tata are waiting for us."

Quietly they made their way, moving from shadow to shadow, trying to be as invisible as possible. Finally, and with much relief, they approached their front yard. Fastened to the lamppost out front was a notice. It read, "There will be a new neighbourhood store opening Saturday morning at ten o'clock." The address was included.

"We have a lot to tell Mama and Tata," exclaimed Halinka as they entered the house.

Later, after Irka had cleaned up and eaten, they sat around the kitchen table, listening to her story.

"Mama and Tata were really scared when they first heard of the war. Then, when talk came of the approaching soldiers, they decided to send me to my grandparents' out in the countryside. I didn't want to go but knew it would be better if I did. Anyway, they hired a man with a wagon to take me. There were kids from other families too. We were to be dropped off at different places. On the way, soldiers stopped us. It was at night. No one could see anything very well. They must have thought the driver was up to no good, because they shot him. The noise of the gun startled me so much that I jumped off the wagon and started running. All the other kids were screaming and crying. I guess the noise distracted the soldiers, because none of them came after me. I hid in the bushes. Then I heard them throw the driver's body off the wagon and drive away. It took me two days and nights to get back to Wolkowysk. I ate raw potatoes from the fields and drank river water, travelling only when it was dark. When I came into town, I tried to go home, but there were too many soldiers. That's when I found the hole. It seemed like a good idea to hide there until it got safer. Fortunately, Therese and Halinka ended up there too. That's how we found each other. Now all I want to do is go home."

"Dear me," said Mama, "it must have been terrible. But now you are safe. We'll see about getting you home as soon as possible."

"Yes," said Tata, "we still have no idea what lies ahead." Mama and Tata looked into each other's eyes. Both of them somehow knew they would need all their faith and strength to get out of this alive.

"Irka, I must take you home tonight. Your parents may have heard about the wagon. They would be terribly worried."

"Yes," agreed Mama, "but she must eat some more first. Come, Irka."

After Irka finished, she and Tata got ready to leave.

"Tata, may I come with you?" asked Halinka.

"Yes, but we must leave at once."

Walking down the deserted and dimly lit streets, it seemed to Halinka that every shadow held a waiting soldier. It was with much relief that she finally saw Irka's house. Tata's rapid knock cut through the silence. The door slowly opened.

Pani gasped when she saw her daughter. "Irka! I'm so glad you are safe!" She pulled her inside with Tata and Halinka close behind.

"Did you hear the news about the wagon?" Tata asked.

Before Pani could respond, Pan came running into the room. "Yes," he answered while taking Irka into his arms. "A villager told us only an hour ago that the wagon had been attacked by soldiers and taken away. It's a miracle she's alive. Thank you so much for bringing her home!"

With Irka safe and reunited with her family, the moment was filled with a sense of joy none of them had felt for a long time.

Chapter Five
THE STORE

At ten o'clock on a cool November evening, everyone was awake, except Helen and Paul. In the kitchen Mama busied herself packing bread and hot tea mixed with honey that had been made by bees kept in the rear yard. Halinka wrapped the bread in a tea towel and then in newspaper. This would keep it warm while Jean and Anne waited in the food line. Mama placed the jar of hot tea in a clean, double-layered, woollen sock and then wrapped it in newspaper as well. It would be a long and cool night waiting for the opening of the new store. Some warm food and hot drinks would be appreciated.

"Mama, what will they be selling at the store?" asked Halinka.

"Who knows, now that the Communists own it," Mama sighed. "We'll have to wait and see."

Tata walked into the room and summoned Jean and Anne. "Remember, both of you will have to wait in line until two o'clock this morning. At that time, I will relieve you. Mama will come at six o'clock. It's best that we take turns. Be very careful, and watch what you say. Most of all, do not talk to the Communists. They may take you away."

"We'll be careful," said Jean.

Therese appeared in the kitchen doorway. "C'mon, Halinka, let's get Jean's and Anne's coats for them."

Minutes later, Jean and Anne, bundled in thick woollen coats, gave everyone hugs as they said goodbye. "God be with you both," said Tata. "We'll be praying."

"Thanks, Tata," replied Jean. The girls opened the door and stepped out into the dark night.

Mama watched the door close behind them. Her one and only hope, and the thought that would consume her for the next few hours, was to see the door open again and their safe return.

Later in bed, Halinka tossed and turned restlessly. The image of her sisters standing outside in the cold wouldn't leave her mind. *I hope they're all right*, she thought. Once more, out of frustration, she fluffed up her down-filled pillow, trying to find a comfortable position. Her mind was filled with thoughts of war, but at long last she dozed off into a fitful sleep.

What seemed like an endless parade of soldiers marched past the front of her house. Without warning, one of them turned and stared at her through the window. Stepping out of line, he began walking toward her. On the way, he reached into his pocket and pulled out a key. It was the house key! Holding it in front of him, he rushed toward the house.

He's coming for me, *she thought. She turned to run away, but her feet wouldn't move. They were stuck to the floor like glue.*

The click of the key turning in the door filled her with panic. She screamed in fear—and suddenly found herself sitting upright in her own bed.

"What's going on?" Therese murmured, stirring from her sleep.

"I was having a horrible dream," said Halinka, her heart still pounding. "A loud clicking noise woke me up."

"That was Tata," explained Therese, now more awake. "I heard him leave for the line."

"That means Jean and Anne should be coming home soon."

"Are you going to stay awake and wait for them?" asked Therese, pulling herself into a sitting position and rubbing the sleep from her eyes.

"Yes." Halinka sighed. "I'm still feeling scared. I hope nothing bad has happened to them."

"I'll stay awake with you." Therese slid closer to her. It was so nice to have an older sister to lean on.

It wasn't long before Jean and Anne could be heard coming through the front door. Therese and Halinka pulled on their knit slippers and dashed out to greet them. Jean and Anne stood inside the doorway, shivering from the cold.

Mama, in her nightgown, prepared warm cups of tea. "I couldn't sleep until I knew you girls were safely home. Here, drink this." She handed them each a cup. "It will help get the chill out of your bones."

"Thanks, Mama," said the girls, reaching for the steaming cups.

As they settled around the kitchen table, Halinka couldn't hold back any longer. "What was it like?" she asked eagerly.

"Cold!" exclaimed Anne. "There was a huge line of people. A lot of our neighbours were there too."

"Some asked about our family," added Jean. "We told them everyone is fine."

"I hope everyone else is doing as well," said Mama softly. "It's awful that we need to line up for so long. Many families are not as fortunate as us." Mama looked lovingly at the girls. It was so wonderful that everyone was willing to do their part. She was grateful. "Thank you for helping. Both of you must be exhausted."

The girls nodded.

"Then that's it," Mama said. "You must drink up and get some rest. Morning will come quickly. I'll need to leave at six o'clock to relieve Tata."

This time when Halinka's head found her pillow, sleep came swiftly. She was confident that Tata could take care of himself.

Late morning sunshine streamed through the curtains. Halinka groggily opened her eyes. *What's that I hear? Am I still dreaming?*

"I'm home, everyone!"

Halinka bolted upright, springing out of bed. Mama had returned home!

It didn't take long for everyone to be awake and standing around Mama, glad to see her safely back and curious to find out what was purchased. Little Helen found her way into Mama's arms.

"Please open the package," Halinka asked eagerly. "We want to know what it is."

When the bag was opened, they were disappointed to find only a half kilogram of flour.

"Is that all?" asked Tata.

"Yes," replied Mama, "but we were fortunate. Those at the end of the line were turned away empty-handed because there was nothing left."

"How will we survive?" asked Jean, echoing the thoughts of the others. Tears welled up in her eyes as she realized how little food was available.

Enduring the Empire

The stores were open only when the army trucks arrived with supplies from Russia. Sometimes a whole week went by. On the night prior to a new store opening, Jean, Anne, Mama, and Tata would take turns standing in line. Waiting through the nights became more difficult as winter approached, and there always seemed to be too little of everything. People wondered what item would be available at each store. It was so unpredictable. Sometimes it was a yard of material or a spool of thread or a food item. Of all the supplies taken out of Poland, only some were bought back. These were now labelled in Russian as if they were actually from Russia. People provided their own sacks, baskets, or boxes to carry what they purchased. Often they would trade amongst themselves.

"Pani Kutsza, what colour of material do you have?" asked a *babcia* (pronounced "bubcha" and meaning "grandma").

"I have blue. Jean has red, and Anne has yellow." On this day the girls had accompanied Mama to the store so they could each get something. This way more of what was needed could be acquired.

"Let's exchange my red for your blue," said the *babcia*. "Then we'll each have enough. It's better to have two metres of the same colour so we can make something useful."

"What a good idea!" Mama replied. And with that, the exchange was made. Now she had enough material to make the fast-growing Helen a new dress.

Rumours were spreading that the Russian army did not like the nighttime lineups. Soon everyone would discover how much.

"It sure is freezing," said Anne, stomping her feet to stay warm one late December night.

"I know," agreed Jean, looking downward and feeling sorry for her sister. She knew how much Anne was suffering from the cold.

A bright light suddenly flashed across a nearby bush. It came from an approaching army truck.

What brings them here at this hour? Jean wondered. She began to feel very uncomfortable.

"Quick, let's hide," she exclaimed, pushing Anne out of the line.

"No!" protested Anne, digging in her heals and pushing back. "We'll lose our place."

"Just do as I say. Look! Get behind this bush." The urgency in her sister's voice prompted Anne to move quickly and duck down low. Others were hastily leaving the line to hide as well, but many stayed.

They peered out from behind their cover. The truck stopped in front of the remaining shoppers. As the cab and rear doors flew open, soldiers jumped out. "You," yelled one, grabbing and yanking a woman out of the line, "get in the back of the truck."

The soldiers continued rounding up the people. Within minutes, the truck was fully loaded and pulling away. When it was out of sight, people cautiously stepped out from their hiding places and formed a new line.

"I hope the soldiers don't return," said a young woman.

"Where did they take them?" someone asked. But no one knew.

Standing in line was a dangerous game to play, yet desperate for supplies, people were willing to take such chances over and over again.

The next day Tata told the girls what had happened to those who were taken. He had heard the news earlier that morning. "They were driven out into the countryside about ten kilometres," he explained.

"Did anyone get hurt?" Halinka asked.

"I'm not sure. They were forced off the truck and made to walk back. Many were cold, hungry, and exhausted, especially the elderly."

Soldiers continued to "catch" people in the line-ups and punish them in this manner. More problems began to surface. One was the lack of money. People didn't have jobs and weren't earning incomes, yet they were expected to buy store items. Mama used some of their reserved food to barter with local farmers so they would have enough to eat. On rare occasions there was even enough milk for everyone to have a full cup.

Before the war, the owner of a local abattoir had a large thriving business that exported meat all over Europe, especially to Germany. Tata often went there to see the owner, Peter, and his family. Returning home, he would bring delicious kolbasa (a Polish sausage), steaks, ground meats, and roasts for everyone to enjoy. Since the Russian takeover, Tata had not attempted to see him.

"Ludwig, would you go and get some meat from Peter?" asked Mama. "We're in need of some. I hope the Russians haven't taken his business." She handed him a full, small sack. "Here, take these potatoes with you to exchange."

An hour later, Tata was back. Deep lines of concern were drawn across his face.

"What is it, Ludwig?" asked Mama.

"They're gone," he whispered in disbelief.

"What do you mean?"

"They're gone—even the business."

He slumped down into a nearby chair, holding his head in his hands, and began to weep.

Halinka rushed to his side. "Oh, Tata, whatever are we going to do?"

Over the passing weeks, food from everyone's fall harvest was still available but not very plentiful. Those who hid extra food had a better chance of making it through the winter. Just the same, meals had to be very carefully rationed. At this point the people were hungry, but not starving—yet.

Chapter Six
A NEW SCHOOL DAY

After the Russian occupation, every school was forced to close. When they reopened some weeks later, many things had changed. Halinka often wondered about her school friends. How were they doing? Would she ever see them again? What about Irka? She missed doing schoolwork, seeing her teachers, and learning with other children.

"Halinka, come quickly," called Mama, peering out the back door. "I've got some good news."

"Coming," said Halinka, jumping off the wooden bench in the back yard. "What is it, Mama?"

"You'll be glad to know the schools are reopening—tomorrow."

"Yippee!" shouted Halinka, jumping up and down. "I'll get my clothes and books ready."

"Bring me anything that needs to be ironed," instructed Mama, smiling at her excitement. The iron always sat on top of the kitchen stove, ready to be heated. It was a triangular shaped piece of heavy steel with a flat bottom and a handle. Mama carefully placed it on the centre of the stove, where it would get hot quickly.

Before long, Halinka arrived with her favourite cotton blouse. The year before, Mama had embroidered it with beautiful flowers and green stems. It had long sleeves with cuffs and a stiff high collar. Now that clothes were so scarce, they were worn as long as possible. Nevertheless, it would look perfect with her green skirt. After Mama ironed the blouse nice and smooth, Halinka hung it in the closet beside the skirt.

Early the next morning after washing up, she proudly donned her outfit. Just as Halinka was putting on her woollen stockings, Therese peeked around the door with a huge grin on her face, "Good morning, Halinka."

"Good morning, Therese. I can hardly wait for school. What about you?"

"I'm sure I can wait longer than you," laughed Therese, tossing her head back. "See you at breakfast."

"Okay. Oh, by the way," Halinka smirked, hands on her hips, "I beat you again."

"Grrr," teased Therese playfully before turning to get herself ready.

"I'll see you later," Halinka said. "Mama told me she'll have something special for us to eat this morning."

As Halinka made her way to the kitchen, the rare smell of freshly baked bread made her glad to know

A New School Day

that Mama still had flour stored in the secret room. The sound of frying eggs reminded her of their only two hens still surviving in the back yard. Up until now, no one had stolen them, for they were kept well out of sight. How long this was going to last, she didn't know, but she was thankful for what was still available.

After breakfast, everyone gathered in the front hall to see the girls off.

"Me too," little Helen asked pleadingly, arms outstretched as the girls gathered up their leather satchels.

"You have to stay here and be with Mama," explained Halinka.

"Come with me, my little one," said Mama, scooping up Helen.

After a brief prayer and some hugs, the girls scurried excitedly out the door. Mama and little Helen watched quietly as they made their way to the schoolyard next door.

It was a large public school for grades one through eight. All the children were there to start their new day. Entering the schoolyard, Halinka noticed the teachers spread out in small groups. Both girls eagerly looked around in hope of finding their teachers.

"There she is," exclaimed Halinka, pointing. "I'd best go to her. See you later, Therese." After a quick embrace, the girls parted.

Halinka hurried over to her teacher. "Hi, Pani Selnik. It's so good to see you again."

"And you too," replied Pani Selnik. "How is your family?"

"Everyone is fine, I guess. I mean, with everything that's going on, things are sure not the same."

"You're right, of course, but please, it is not a thing to discuss ... this war and the occupation." She glanced over her shoulder nervously. "I have found out there are listening ears all around us. We must choose our words carefully lest we bring trouble upon ourselves and our families. Oh, look," she changed the subject, "here come some of your classmates."

Coming their way was a group of smiling, familiar faces. The small mob surrounded her, and the next thing she knew, they were all dancing around, laughing and hugging each other. How good it was to be together again!

A loud roar from the nearby roadside brought the happy gathering to a standstill. Russian army trucks were pulling up in front of the school. With screeching brakes, one stopped right in front of them. A uniformed man yelled for everyone's attention. Smiling, he told them they would be driven around the town "Russian style" to celebrate their new way of life.

Before she knew it, Halinka was suddenly lifted up into the back of the truck. Peering over the side, she saw Therese's terrified expression as she too was picked up. The same thing was happening to all the other children. *How can we trust our enemy?* Halinka wondered. *How can we know for sure we'll be brought back? What if we're really being taken to Russia?*

"Halinka," a faraway voice called out.

As she scanned the surrounding faces, her eyes found Irka, who was waving to get her attention. She was at the other end of the same truck!

"Therese, come on; it's Irka." Holding hands, Therese and Halinka began to squeeze through the crowd. When they finally reached Irka, they all fell into each other's arms, just as the truck lurched forward.

"Wow, it's so great to see the two of you!" Irka gasped in obvious relief.

"We've been really missing you too."

This unexpected surprise warmed Halinka's heart, and she revelled in the joy of the moment. It did not last long, for it was interrupted by the sound of many soldiers bursting forth loudly in song. *A Russian victory song*, she mused.

The soldiers in the truck with them waved their hands and nodded their heads to encourage their captive audience to join in. It was certainly not something Halinka wanted to do, and she was sure her schoolmates felt the same way. Gradually, and with obvious reluctance, the children joined in, singing what words they could understand.

The trip through Wolkowysk lasted about an hour. As soon as the trucks arrived back at the schoolyard, the soldiers began helping the children out of the trucks. This brought much relief to Halinka, but out of the corner of her eye she saw that the soldiers' faces were once again serious. Their earlier happy expressions were only a facade, trying to convince everyone that all was well.

The children were then sent home, thus bringing their first day at school to an abrupt end. Halinka wondered what tomorrow would bring. The war had changed so many things.

After breakfast the following morning, Mama walked the girls to school. "I'll see you later," she said, hugging them just as the school bell began to ring. Cautiously, the girls went to their assigned classes.

After finding a seat, Halinka was quick to notice a large, new picture on the front wall. Where there once hung a crucifix, there now was a strange man's picture. *Who is this man?* she wondered. There was something about him that she did not like. Later she would find out that his name was Joseph Stalin, their new Communist leader.

"Class, please stand up," said the teacher as she made her way to her desk.

A New School Day

Halinka was always glad to see Pani Selnik. She had learned the morning routine last September, so she expected the first order of the day to be the saying of the Lord's Prayer. Instead, the teacher, who did not act very enthusiastic, announced they would be learning a new song. Just as they began to sing, a man walked in and stood watching from the back of the room. *Who is he? Why is he here?*[7]

They soon found out that such individuals had been sent out to ensure everything was done exactly the way Stalin ordered. Teachers who refused to cooperate would be punished by having their jobs taken away or, even worse, being sent to a work camp.

"Please repeat the lines after me," the teacher continued. Halinka sang loudly with her classmates, each of them struggling to pronounce the words. At the end of the song, they were instructed to take out their own personal blackboards. Each blackboard fit perfectly in their schoolbags. Attached to the boards by two strings were a small sponge and a cloth. These were used for erasing and cleaning. It was every child's responsibility

---

[7] Halinka would later learn the meaning of the words to the songs. One example was "Not a tsar, not a god, and not a man of wealth. We get our blessings with our own hands." Everything taught was geared to change everyone's thinking and get them to believe in the communist way of life. In reality, the Communists had no use for people's individual rights. Anyone who objected was considered an enemy and was either punished or put to death.

to wash his or her blackboard daily and make sure the sponge was damp each morning before school.

Pani Selnik began. "Today you will begin to learn the Russian alphabet."

As Halinka watched and imitated drawing each letter, she was surprised at how different they looked from the Polish alphabet. They worked on the alphabet throughout the day, and most of the time the teacher only spoke in Russian. This was to speed up the learning process.

At recess, Halinka noticed many teachers huddled together and speaking in hushed tones. It only happened when the mysterious visitor was gone.

Later that evening at home, Halinka spoke with Therese. "What a different school day it was: no crucifix on the wall, we didn't say prayers, and we didn't sing any hymns! What we did do was learn some new songs in Russian and the Russian alphabet. At the front of the class there is now a picture of a man. Pani Selnik told us his name is Joseph Stalin, the ruler of Russia. I really don't like the way he looks. He seemed to be staring at me all day long."

"Your day sounds a lot like mine," said Therese. "I don't care for that picture either. The teacher told us they all have to follow new laws because we are now under communist rule. They said the Russian language has to be taught and the communist songs have to be sung. It's also now against the law to say the Lord's Prayer or talk of God. Instead of saying the Lord's Prayer, we're supposed to greet that Stalin man."

Over supper, as the girls talked about their day, Mama and Tata listened intently. At one point, Tata firmly stated, "There will be no communist songs sung in this home."

Over and over again, people heard the new government boasting "Poland is now free." The Polish people, however, wondered to themselves, "Free from what?"

"Yes," they would say, "we're free all right. Free from enough food and money, from jobs, from owning possessions, and from religion." This was not freedom. The new government had taken almost everything away from them. As far as Halinka was concerned, the Communists had stolen their freedom.

What would happen next?

Chapter Seven
WARTIME CHRISTMAS

Christmas Eve eventually arrived and, with it, no peace. The war was intensifying, but even so, Mama and Tata tried to make it as special as possible. The Christmas tree looked beautiful, adorned with paper angels the girls had made earlier that afternoon from old tissue paper. Everyone helped Mama get the evening meal ready. Even Tata peeled potatoes. Jean was busy at the stove, stirring a pot full of fruit with a hand-carved wooden spoon. She had just added water to the pear, apple, and plum mixture known as compote (pronounced "com-put").

"This compote sure smells good," she exclaimed, inhaling the sweet aroma.

"I agree," said Anne, pulling the pan of platski (a form of potato pancakes) from the oven, "but mine smells better." Smirking, she playfully elbowed Jean in the back as she walked by.

"Helen," called Halinka, "do you see the first star outside yet? We're getting hungry."

Their Polish tradition held true. No one ate until the first star appeared in the evening sky. Didn't the wise men see a star in the east before they found the home of Jesus? So it was that many families kept this tradition all over Poland. In remembrance of that first Christmas long ago, the star had to appear prior to them celebrating.

"No star," Helen sighed sadly, shaking her head. Perched on the couch, gazing intently upward, she waited eagerly for the first glimmer of light.

"How much food is on the table now?" Therese asked.

"One, two, three ... nine," Halinka replied. The kitchen table was neatly set with Mama's good china. Lead crystal glasses shimmered in the candlelight like diamonds all aglow.

"We still need two more dishes, plus dessert."

Following another tradition, twelve items of food were put on the table to represent each one of Jesus' twelve disciples.

"Here's the compote." Jean placed the steaming fruit dish on the table.

"And here are the mashed potatoes," announced Anne, emerging from the kitchen.

"Come and sit down, everyone," instructed Tata.

At that moment a loud screech of delight caused everyone to jump. It was Helen.

"First star, first star," she shouted, jumping up and down and clapping her hands.

"Good for you, Helen," Mama chuckled. "Come and sit down. Thanks to you, we can begin our meal."

Helen quickly scrambled off the couch, eager to join the others. Halinka looked around the table. She first noticed the fish cousin Zigmund had caught in the river earlier that day. They all knew no meat could be eaten on Christmas Eve.[8]

In addition to the fish, there were mashed potatoes with lard-based gravy, compote, baked sauerkraut, carrots and beans from their fall harvest, platski, wild mushrooms stuffed in pierogies, pickled beets, and freshly baked bread. Apple cake would be served later for dessert. Although there was only very little of each, it amounted to much when put together. Mama was good at stretching out food, and Tata, on this special occasion, did allow a little more to be eaten than usual. Who knew what next Christmas would bring?

Everyone joined hands around the table and began singing "Silent Night" in remembrance of Christ's birth. After this, the communion bread was passed around. Tata said a short prayer and encouraged everyone to be thankful.

---

8 The absence of meat was to remind them of the animals around the manger when Jesus was born in Bethlehem.

"Remember," he said, "God will never leave us nor forsake us, no matter what happens."

No encouragement was needed to "dig in" and eat. Halinka especially loved the pierogies. Normally Mama would stuff the pasta shells with potatoes and cheese or sauerkraut. However, tonight they had the added flavour of wild mushrooms picked from the nearby forest.

When they had finished eating, Mama left the table and returned with a small armful of gifts. Beaming with delight, she called out for each of them to receive their presents. "I hope you like them," she exclaimed.

They were all new! There had not been anything new for so long. Everyone received a pair of hand-knit mittens. Mama had worked many hours in secret to get them made in time.

"Where did you get the wool?" asked Halinka.

"I purchased it long before the war started, when it was still available. I am so glad there was enough to make something for each of you."

As Halinka hugged hers closely to her chest she was reminded of her mother's love. *What a wonderful Christmas*! Even her belly felt full for a change.

Chapter Eight
DISAPPEARANCES

By mid-January, the weather had turned bitterly cold. The girls bundled up in scarves, hats, boots, and, of course, their new mittens. A fresh blanket of snow fell over the town one night, settling on trees and buildings like fluffy, white cotton. The crunching sound of boots, which revealed the frosty cold of the morning, could be heard as Therese and Halinka walked to school.

Noticing yet another house void of occupants, Halinka exclaimed, "Look, Therese, another empty house! Where is everyone going?"

"I really don't know," Therese responded. "I've heard that some people have run to the west away from the Russians."

"Well, I heard Tata say many people have run from the west and come east to escape the Germans." Halinka looked down, shaking her head. "Nobody seems to know where to go. Why does everyone want to take our country away from us? Why can't they just leave us alone?"

"As far as I can figure," said Therese, "the Russians want us to be part of Russia, and the Germans want us to be part of Germany."

Halinka noticed a padlock on the door of a deserted home. There was a note attached. "What is that, Therese?" she asked, pointing at the house.

"I don't know, but let's find out."

At the door, Therese leaned over and read it aloud. "This building is now owned by the Russian government." She thought for a moment. "I'll bet they didn't pay for it, either. But why is no one here?"

They stared at the paper for a moment, trying to understand what it meant or if it would affect their own lives. "We'll ask Tata when we get home from school," said Halinka. "He knows almost everything. Come on." She grabbed Therese by the hand.

"You're right. Let's go quickly, or we'll be late."

Later, after school, the girls hurried to get home. They did not stop and chat with friends as usual. The disappearance of so many people weighed heavy on their minds.

"Hi, Mama. Hi, Tata," called Halinka as she opened the door to their home.

"Hi, Mama. Hi, Tata," echoed Therese.

They found their parents seated in the kitchen.

"How come so many of our classmates are not at school anymore?" asked Halinka.

"Yes, it's true," added Therese, "and today I noticed Ted and Anna Zolek were missing. So was John Jenski."

"Not only that," said Halinka, "we went for a closer look at a deserted home. On the door was a padlock with a metal seal. There was Russian writing engraved on it."

Mama and Tata grew serious, their faces filled with concern. "We have been told," Tata began, "that the Russians are loading people on freight trains and shipping them to Siberia."

The girls gasped. Tata continued, "The lock and seal you found on that house was put there by the new government. It means they have already taken that family away."

"Why?" asked Jean, who had just arrived and was listening to the conversation.

"It is because the Communists are against the wealthy, academics, and anyone that could be considered a threat. They raid houses at night when everyone is asleep. Today I found out that the mayor and his family are gone. They have also taken many of our doctors and lawyers and their families."

"That's awful," declared Halinka.

"They think everyone should be equal in all ways," said Mama. "To them, the rich take what they want from the poor. Yet they come and take whatever they want but only give back a little, or nothing."

"Tata," Halinka asked, her voice becoming very soft, "last night I woke up hearing animal noises from the freight trains sitting in the railyard. It sounded like cows mooing or something. Are they loading them up at night?"

"Honey," Tata's voice cracked, "those were the sounds of people suffering."

Everyone was silent. The image of people loaded on freight cars like cattle was so disturbing. Halinka felt a deep pang of sorrow in her heart. Tears welled up in everyone's eyes at the thought of such horrible treatment.

Finally, Anne blurted out, "What about us? Are they going to take us too?"

"I don't know," he replied. "Not if I can help it. I am going downtown tomorrow to speak secretly with a local official and come up with a plan."

Over the next few weeks, many freight trains travelled through Wolkowysk. People from all over eastern Poland were being taken away to Siberia. Halinka didn't know much about the place other than that it was very far away, very cold, and very desolate. There was little chance of anyone surviving, either on the trip or when they arrived.[9]

There was a knock on the door.

"I'll get it," said Halinka, who was already hurrying away.

"Irka," said Halinka, hugging her friend, "I'm so glad you've come for a visit."

Earlier in the day, Tata had met with Irka's father. They had carefully made arrangements to get the families together. It had been a long time.

"Me too," said Irka, smiling warmly. "Do you think the Russians are going to take us away too? I mean, it's happened to so many people already."

"I hope not," said Halinka. "Come on, let's have a game of pig and not think about these things."[10]

---

9   It has been estimated that over the course of the war, roughly one million Polish people were sent to Siberia in this manner. The following is typical of what it was like on one of these trains: Selected people (from fifty to eighty per car) were put on board, and the doors were locked from the outside. They would travel for weeks to their destination with no opportunity to wash or walk around. They did receive a daily ration in an attempt to keep most of them alive, but it was usually only a piece of bread and some thin cabbage soup.

10 By now hundreds of captive people were coming through town weekly on freight trains headed for the Russian frontier. Many of their neighbours and friends had already been taken. It was only a matter of time ...

For the next hour the girls laughed and giggled, thoroughly enjoying each other's company. The war seemed a million miles away. Later, after tea, Pan announced that it was time for them to go. All too soon, this special occasion together was over. Saying goodbye was difficult, because everyone knew it could be their last.

By the middle of March, the food supply had dwindled considerably. Mama desperately needed milk for Paul, so one evening she announced, "I must go out of town to get some goat's milk for Paul. Halinka, would you like to come with me?"

"I sure would," answered Halinka eagerly, wanting to get out of the house again.

Walking silently down the dark, deserted streets, they noticed the many vacant homes. Thinking about why they were empty made Halinka shudder. Unconsciously she pulled her coat tighter around herself. As they made their way past Pan and Pani Kowalski's home, she wondered where they could be. It was a relief to see that no government seal was on their door.

When they arrived at the farm, Mama exchanged some flour for goat's milk. After a brief conversation, much of which was about the war, they thanked the farmer and began the journey back home.

As they approached the street where the Kowolskis lived, Halinka grabbed Mama's hand and gasped, "Mama, look!"

They could see an army truck parked outside the house. No one appeared to be in or around the vehicle. A movement from inside the house caught their attention. Pani suddenly appeared in the large front window. She was running around the living room, pulling down her beautiful curtains. Her screams could be heard even from where Halinka and Mama were walking on the far side of the street. Then, without warning, she was grabbed by two Russian soldiers and dragged out of sight.

"We must leave quickly, Halinka. There is nothing we can do." Mama began to run, pulling her along. Behind them they heard Pani's screams get louder as she was brought outside and taken to the waiting truck.

They felt so helpless. Tears streamed down their faces. Fear of getting caught themselves drove them to run all the way home.

"Mama," gasped Halinka as they neared their front door, "did they take Irka too?" Afterwards, they found out that Pani and Pan had been taken away separately. Later, Pani escaped and ran back home. As she began ripping down all her curtains, the soldiers arrived. It was then that Mama and Halinka happened on the scene.[11]

Wolkowysk actually had two train stations, one for passenger trains and one for freight trains. Halinka's home was located only a short distance from the main freight train station. The town prided itself in being part of an extensive rail system that connected much of Europe to Asia. It was an important junction that cost the country a great deal of money to build and maintain. For example, passengers and freight could travel all the way to France, pass through Wolkowysk and on to Russia, or exchange trains and go to Lithuania.

At one time Tata had worked as a police officer. Part of his duty was guarding an eight kilometre stretch of tracks on the outskirts of town. Later, he worked as a private investigator until he was shot in the leg. He never fully recovered from the wound. Although he remained with the local police force, he was limited to working in the office.

---

[11] Both Pan and Pani were shipped to Siberia. Neither was ever heard from again.

Chapter Nine
THE BLACK LIST

Twice over the next two days, Tata searched for Irka. It was important that he not be seen by any army patrols. He concentrated mostly in the area of her neighbourhood, believing she had not gone very far. Still, there was no sign of her.

There was another possibility as to why she had not yet been located, but no one wanted to consider it.

Halinka and Therese prayed for their friend and constantly discussed her possible whereabouts.

"Maybe she's hiding in the woods," ventured Therese.

"I doubt it," Mama said. "There are always soldiers with dogs out there, trying to find members of the Resistance. She would be aware of this and know they would find her. No, there must be another place."[12]

---

[12] The Polish Resistance movement in World War II was the largest underground resistance in all of Nazi-occupied Europe. It was most effective in disrupting German supply lines, providing intelligence, and saving more Jewish lives than any other allied organization.

A shout interrupted their conversation. It was Anne. "Therese, Halinka, come and set the table. We're almost ready to eat."

As they made their way to the kitchen, they were still pondering and discussing Irka's possible whereabouts. When they entered, Anne was speaking to Jean. "Tata left to go somewhere with Zigmund early this morning. They were going to pick up our new identification papers."

"Did Tata say how long they would be gone?" asked Jean.

"They will try to be back sometime this afternoon."

Halinka and Therese began scraping together a meal of potato pancakes while listening to their sisters.

Halinka noticed that the potatoes were sprouting all over. They were shrivelled and wrinkled and reminded her of old, weather-beaten faces.

"Yuk! Are you using these rotten potatoes?" she asked Therese, pointing to some mushy ones nearby.

"Yes, I was told to cut off the bad parts and use whatever good parts are left."

Nothing was wasted. By this time, all their fruits, beans, preserved goods, and meats were used up. Only a handful of old and rotting potatoes, two carrots, a few apples, some sauerkraut, and a small amount of flour remained. These would not go very far, perhaps only a few more days.

Halinka recalled Nini's words of what seemed like so long ago: "Someday you may even wish to have the bacon you're feeding Rex." How true those words were today! Halinka's stomach ached from hunger. Her heart also ached, knowing that her family and many others were experiencing the same thing. Even poor Rex—she glanced over to where he lay. *What will become of him if this crazy war continues?* Tears welled up in her eyes. Rex slowly got up and, as though sensing her pain, came and rested his head in her lap. She reached down and gave him a big hug. How she loved this dog!

The front door suddenly opened, and Mama entered with the day's rations.

"What great feast do we have today?' asked Jean sarcastically.

"Two hundred grams of sugar," Mama replied, placing it on the table.

"Yummy, yummy," squealed Helen as she ran for the table.

She sure misses having sweets, thought Halinka. Sugar had become very rare.

"Well, already one good thing for today," said a smiling Therese.

"Yes," agreed Mama, "and we must be sure to count our blessings, no matter how small."

Halinka looked around the room. She was so thankful that her family was still together. *Poor Irka, her parents have been taken away. Where could she be?*

The noise of a door opening behind her brought her out of her deep thoughts. It was Tata. As he entered the kitchen, he fixed his eyes on Mama. "Olga," he said, his voice filled with alarm, "I met with Pan Zolski. He told me he saw our names on the black list. Our family is next in line to be put on a freight train for Siberia—tonight! We must leave right away."

Halinka's heart began beating wildly as the meaning of the news sunk in. Letting out a sigh, Mama fainted in a heap onto the floor.

"Mama," Halinka screamed.

Tata, Jean, and Anne rushed to help.

"Come on, Halinka," said Therese, "let's take Helen and Paul out of here so Tata can help Mama. We'll take them to our room." They scooped them up and carried them out of the kitchen and down the hall.

It seemed like a long time later, but finally Tata's voice could be heard calling for everyone to meet in the kitchen. "Children, Mama will be fine. She fainted because of the unexpected news. However, now we must act quickly. Listen very carefully. I have new identification papers here that will allow us to travel west, where the Germans have territorial control."[13]

"Why are we going there?" asked Halinka.

"I believe we have a better chance of survival with the Germans than with the Russians." Tata continued, "If we stay here, we will be sent to Siberia with little or no chance of survival. After spending much time in prayer, I believe this is our only hope.

"Our identity has been changed. We are no longer Polish Kutsza but, rather, German Kutsche." He held up a stack of papers.

"These official documents will prove to the Germans that we are of German descent. No one is to know I worked for the Polish government in the police department. If they find out, they will take me away and probably kill me. They may do the same to you. From now on we must only use our new name,

---

[13] The Nazi-Soviet pact that was signed on August of 1939 was called the Molotov-Ribbentrop pact. It was part of the non-aggression pact between Hitler and Stalin. They agreed that after each had taken over their half of Poland, both German and Russian people would be allowed to return to their land of ancestry, regardless of which side they were on.

Kutsche, and if anyone asks, your father is an industrial mechanic. Do not say anything else."[14]

Tata did not want the family to know or try to remember too much detail. He knew they could not be made to reveal what they did not know if they were caught.

Walking to the far side of the kitchen, Tata opened up one of the cupboard drawers and removed some papers. They were his old identification documents. "I need to burn these so the Russians won't find them," he said, walking over to the stove. Halinka noticed a photo of him in a police uniform. How handsome he looked.

As Tata opened the door of the stove, a knock was heard at the door. Everyone froze, except Tata, who quickly threw the papers into the fire and sealed up the stove.

"Ludwig! Olga! Open up. It's Zigmund and Auntie." They had come to help them get ready. Tata's farmer friend, Marek, would drive them to the station

---

14 None of this was a lie. When he was younger, his father had been such a mechanic and taught him much of the trade. Tata was confident he knew enough about it to pass as a tradesman to the Germans. Such a skill was useful in their war effort. As for changing the name to German, the family was aware that although Tata was born in Poland, they did have some German ancestry. An added asset was that he could fluently speak Polish, Russian, German, and Yiddish.

where they would board the train that would carry them westward.

Mama raced to the door, opened it, and threw her arms around Auntie. "I'm so glad you've come," she sobbed.

The next hour flew by like a whirlwind. Everything happened so quickly. Mama and Tata gave everyone some instructions and a basket. Some would hold what little food was left, and others a few personal belongings and blankets for each of them. Only two items of clothing and a coat were allowed per person. Jean was put in charge of bringing the hand mirror and some family pictures. While all this was happening inside, Zigmund and Auntie were outside preparing the horse and wagon. When everything was ready, they would leave to catch a train leaving from the other side of town.

The girls were upstairs getting prepared.

"I can't even think," said Halinka with a sigh.

"I know how you feel," agreed Therese. "I can't either."

"Just pick two favourite things that are warm," advised Anne.

Halinka finally chose a long-sleeved blue blouse and grey leggings as her clothing. As they began to leave, she stopped at the door to take a last look. Sadly, she gazed at the beautiful white feather quilt lying on her bed. Her grandma had made it especially for her. It hurt that she could not bring it along. *Will I ever see any of this again?*

As Halinka entered the kitchen a few minutes later, she noticed how worried Mama looked. She knew it was hard for Mama to let it all go. Everything here was a part of their lives. Only the memories they could carry in their hearts and minds would stay with them forever.

The sound of the back door opening caught everyone's attention. It was Tata and Zigmund, who had finished getting the wagon ready. "It's time to go," said Tata.

"Gather up everything, children," ordered Mama.

Halinka looked at her beloved Rex lying quietly in the corner of the kitchen, his head resting on his paws. He looked up with sad eyes. Was he sensing they were leaving for good? One by one they each hugged their devoted dog. This excited him, and he sat up, his tail wagging frantically. When it was Halinka's turn she crouched down and clung tightly to Rex's neck. The ache in her felt so deep and endless.

"I love you, Rex," she sobbed. He whimpered and licked at the stream of tears rolling down her face. She didn't want to let go of him. What would become of him? *Will he survive or become another victim in this terrible war?* "Lord, please look after him for us," was all she could say.

Gently, Mama touched Halinka's shoulder. "It is time to go now," she said, her voice quivering with emotion. She too hated the thought of leaving. Stooping down to pick up the picnic basket, Halinka suddenly froze.

"Tata," she screamed, running outside, "I know where Irka is hiding!"

"What? What are you saying?" Tata asked, turning to face her.

"Remember when we brought Irka home, the time she escaped from the wagon?"

"Yes," Tata replied, beginning to realize where this was leading.

"If I know her, she's gone back to that same hiding place. There was a basket there too. That's what made me remember. Please, can I go and get her?"

"Halinka, the Russians are coming for us! They will be here soon."

"But Tata, she mustn't be left behind. Please! I promise I won't be long!"

Inwardly, he prayed for direction. Looking into his daughter's eyes, he saw the love she had for her friend and the deep determination to see her safe. "All right, Halinka," he said with resignation, "but you must promise to be back within twenty minutes, no longer, whether you find her or not!"

"Thanks, Tata! I promise. I'll be careful too." She grabbed her coat and bolted out the front door.

Upon reaching the street, she stopped and looked closely in every direction. *Good, there are no soldiers or trucks.* She ran as fast as she could toward the hiding place, glancing occasionally over her shoulder and expecting to hear the shout of pursuing soldiers at any time. All the while she pleaded within herself, *Please, Irka, be there!* By the time she arrived, her lungs burned from the effort. Behind the familiar bush at the entrance hole she collapsed on her hands and knees, heaving for breath. With a weary but determined effort she yanked open the small trap door.

"Irka, Irka," she gasped, peering down into the darkness.

Nothing!

Chapter Ten
A TIME TO SAY GOODBYE

With only the silent blackness staring up at her, Halinka's hope began to fade. All she wanted to do now was cry.

"Halinka." The voice was faint and barely audible. "Is that ... is that you?"

Am I hearing things?

"Help me ... please."

"Irka?" asked Halinka.

"Yes, it's me."

"You're safe! Oh, Irka, I'm so sorry about your parents. I've come to help you. Please come up. Hurry, we must get to my place quickly. The Russians are coming for my family too. Tata has a plan to escape. You'll be safe!"

A hand suddenly appeared. Grabbing on tightly, Halinka pulled and watched in relief as her friend emerged.

"There's no time to talk now," she said as they embraced.

Irka felt so cold. She had been hiding for two days and nights in a cold and dark hole in the ground.

Halinka led them between two houses and onto a back street. "This way," she whispered. The way looked clear.

Because Irka was so weak, they couldn't travel very fast. The sound of their feet on the cobblestone streets echoed beneath them. It seemed so loud.

"Just two more streets to go," encouraged Halinka as they turned another corner.

Without warning, the darkness ahead was lit up.

"It's a truck!" Halinka shouted. The girls dashed behind a nearby tree, praying they hadn't been spotted. They listened as the truck drove by and came to a stop. Risking a look, they saw it was only five houses away. With horror, they watched as three soldiers disembarked. Two remained by the truck with guns ready; the other went and pounded on the front door. There was no response, so he proceeded to smash it in with the butt of his rifle. He entered, and the others immediately followed. Their voices could be heard screaming commands at whoever was inside, ordering them to get ready to leave.

"What do we do?" asked Irka. The fear in her voice mirrored Halinka's own feelings.

Are these same soldiers coming for us? Halinka wondered. *Will we make it home on time?*

Minutes later, they watched as a lady carrying a small child was roughly pushed by one of the soldiers to the rear of the truck and ordered to climb aboard. He was facing away from Halinka and Irka, and the others had not yet appeared. Halinka knew it was time to leave.

"Now," she grabbed Irka by the arm, "let's go!" They began to run as quietly as possible along the side of the street, expecting at any moment to hear a shout or a shot from a rifle. After what seemed like forever, they rounded a corner and were out of sight. There was only one block to go.

Please God, don't let them come yet. Halinka feared the Russians might beat them to the house or, worse, already be there with another truck.

Gradually, out of the darkness the faint outline of her family wagon came into view. Everyone was sitting, nervously waiting for their arrival. The scuffling of their feet on the cobblestone drive caused them to turn and look in their direction. "Hurry up," Therese called, waving her arms frantically.

"Hush," said Tata, not wanting to attract any attention.

"Tata, I found her," Halinka panted breathlessly, reaching up for his outstretched arms.

"Oh, I am so glad." He pulled her up and hugged her close. "You've been a brave little girl."

Mama jumped down from the wagon and brought Irka, who seemed to be in a daze, to Auntie Anne.

"Come with me, Irka," said Auntie Anne softly, taking her in her arms. "We'll take care of you. In a few days we too will have the necessary papers to leave."

"Giddy-up," said Marek, slapping the reins, sending a signal to the horses that it was time to go. The wagon lurched forward. Halinka and Irka looked at each other. They wanted so much to see one another again.

As they pulled away from their house, Mama whispered, "Wave goodbye to your home, children. We may never see it again." With great sadness they waved one last time and then sprawled out to make themselves as comfortable as possible.

"I hope to see you soon," Halinka called out from between her cupped hands. There were tears running down her face.

"Me too," came the faint reply, and then they were gone from sight.

Everyone was quiet, lost in their own thoughts. Halinka looked up at the stars shining brilliantly in the clear, cold night. *How beautiful!* They were so far away from every earthly trouble. She was glad they would be gone when the Russians invaded their home. It was frightening to think of being put on a freight train to Siberia. *Tata was right; it is better to take this risk.*

Travelling west toward the train station, a sense of hope rose up within her. No matter what the future held for her family, it was in God's hands. They needed a miracle, and with the miracle they would stay together and fight to survive.

Sadly, Irka and her parents were never seen again by any of the Kutsche family. Her last known location was at her grandparents' home in the Polish countryside. From this point they never received any knowledge of whether or not she escaped, was caught and sent to Siberia, or died.

Fellow citizens of Wolkowysk, whom the family connected with later in the war, told them what happened at their home. The same night that the family departed, a group of Russian soldiers surrounded their place. This extra manpower and tactics were used because Halinka's father was known to them as one who had served in the government police force. They were concerned about the possibility of armed resistance. When no one responded to the order to come out, they blasted the house with machine gun fire. They were very angry to later discover it was deserted.

Book Two
WELCOME TO THE THIRD REICH

"You prepare a table before me in the presence of my enemies."

—Psalm 23:5a

PROLOGUE

Empire! How magnificent that word sounds! Ruling over many states and countries would be supreme power! Nothing could be greater.

Germany was a country of long ago, traced back to the Roman commander Julius Caesar, who referred to the unconquered region east of the Rhine River as Germania.

THE FIRST REICH

In 800 A.D., the German nation became the Holy Roman Empire, ushering in the birth of the First Reich. Some say it began in 843 A.D., on Christmas Day, when Charles the Great (Charlemagne) was crowned Emperor by Pope Leo III in Rome. Others say it began when Otto I was crowned in 962 A.D. Regardless, this empire lasted throughout the medieval period until 1806.

This was a period of great and tumultuous change, from feudal systems in agricultural lands, with peasants, nobles, knights, clergymen, and kings, to no feudal systems, with the founding of universities in rising towns and cities. It was marked by famines, wars, and plagues, including the Black Death, which killed about a third of all Europeans. It was also a time of religious reformation, spurred by Martin Luther, who headed the reformation from Catholic to Protestant Christianity. In 1806, when Emperor Francis II was no longer in power, the First Reich ceased to exist.

THE SECOND REICH

Germany once again became an empire in 1871 after the Franco-Prussian War. Wilhelm I was crowned as Germany's emperor at the Palace of Versailles.

The country grew and changed through the Industrial Revolution and the springing up of world class universities for science and the humanities. It became the dominant power on the European continent, so much so that by 1900, its industrial economy surpassed Britain's, ushering in a naval race and aggressive strategy on how it dealt with other countries. Greater power was on Germany's agenda, which led to World War I.

After that war, from 1920 to 1930, a defeated, economically crippled, and partly occupied Germany had no emperor, king, or prince. The country was forced to pay war reparations to other countries according to the Treaty of Versailles. All that was left for leadership was an unstable parliamentary democracy, the Weimar Republic.

Then, in the early 1930s, the worldwide Great Depression hit, and Germany spiralled into an even greater devastation. Unemployment soared, food was scarce, and people lost confidence in the government.

THE THIRD REICH

In 1933, a new empire began to emerge, the Third Reich, under one supreme authority. It was a totalitarian regime that promised to make Germany great again. Any political figures opposed to the movement were quickly killed or imprisoned by the new leader, Adolf Hitler, and his party, the Nazi Party. Hitler was unstoppable, and the economy quickly improved as jobs for public works and armaments appeared. People's dignity and hopes were also renewed, but his deception would cost the nation greatly. This new leader was not an emperor.

Chapter Eleven
THE TRAIN RIDE

"Clip, clop, clip, clop..." The steady rhythm of the horses' hooves and slowly enveloping darkness gently lulled Halinka to sleep. Her home town of Wolkowysk, along with everything she had known for the first ten years of her life, now seemed a million miles away. World War II had been raging for nine months, and all of Poland was under Russian or German control. She and her family were now heading west.

It was early morning, and the orange glow of the sun peered over the horizon. Throughout the night they had travelled many back roads to reach their new destination.

"*Stoy!*" a Russian voice suddenly bellowed.

Marek pulled on the reigns so abruptly, Halinka was immediately awake. Lying as still as a stone, she listened intently. *What will happen next?*

The Russian guard motioned for Marek to pull over and stop.

By now, Therese was stirring. Gently, Halinka placed her hand on Therese's shoulder and whispered, "Shhh. Don't speak too loudly."

"Halinka, are we at the train station?" Therese inquired.

"Yes, I think so."

"Girls, we are going to board a train here," Mama spoke quietly. "It will take us to the new German-Russian border. Everyone with German ancestry can board and leave this Russian occupied section of Poland. Be sure to stay close to Tata and I, and pray for the Lord's protection."

Halinka slid her blanket to one side, sat up, and gave a big yawn.

"Papers!" another guard ordered.

Tata handed an envelope to one of two Russian guards while the other climbed up the side of the wagon and peered inside. His plain, brown uniform looked dismal against the dim morning light. On his sleeve, a bright red badge displayed a white hammer and sickle.

I must ask Tata what those symbols mean.

Suddenly, the guard spotted the picnic basket on Halinka's lap. "Be sure to take all the food you can, little one. There is no food in Germany! You are going to the wrong side!" He laughed as he continued his inspection. Finally, the guards seemed satisfied that all was in order. To Halinka's relief, papers were handed back to Tata, and they were waved on.

The guard's words swirled around in her mind: "No food in Germany" and "You are going to the wrong side!" *Could it be true? What would they do?* She dared not believe him!

Halinka looked down at her picnic basket and lifted the corner of the covering cloth. Inside were the hardened crusts of bread Mama had carefully dried in the oven. As Mama had explained, bread prepared in this manner would last much longer because of its dryness. The moisture in soft bread attracted bacteria, which created mold very quickly. Cheese, boiled eggs, and a few dried prunes also lay among the two jars of peppermint and chamomile tea.

"Thank goodness he didn't take our food," Therese sighed.

"I don't believe what he said!" exclaimed Halinka. "There must be food in Germany!"

"He's just being mean and trying to make us afraid," Therese said. "Tata wouldn't take us to a place without food."

"True," agreed Halinka, "he loves us too much."

Marek turned the wagon around so they could disembark.

"I cannot thank you enough for what you have done for us," Tata said to his friend.

Marek smiled. "Finally, I am able to repay you!"[15]

"All right, everyone," announced Tata, "it's time to get off. Follow me, and please remain quiet. I will do the talking."

After unloading, Marek waved one last goodbye and drove away.

The family carried their belongings to a waiting passenger train and boarded. Everyone sat down on the benches inside the rail car, with their baskets, suitcases, and sacks strewn around them. It was nothing like the luxury trains with their plush seats and overhead baggage compartments.

The economy class passenger train ran on the smaller gauge tracks. Most of Europe, including Germany and Poland, used this smaller standard gauge, and Russia used the broader gauge tracks. Later in the war, Germany's efforts to conqueror the Soviet Union were complicated by having different rail gauges.

"Mama, I need to go to the washroom," Halinka whispered. She wondered where she would be able to go.

---

[15] A number of years earlier, when Tata was on the police force, he worked on a case that involved Marek, who had been falsely accused of a crime. During the investigation, Tata discovered evidence that resulted in the charge being dropped. Marek never forgot what Tata had done for him.

Thankfully, Mama had noticed a small washroom when they entered the railcar.

"Halinka," she said, pointing toward the end of the car, "you will find one over there."

Halinka was relieved. She remembered hearing that there were no washrooms on the freight trains bound for Siberia, and that people were crammed like sardines in a can with no place to sit. Tata was right. Heading west was better than heading east.

When she returned, Halinka nestled in beside Tata.

"Tata, what do the hammer and sickle mean on the Russian uniforms?"

"After the Czar was removed from power and killed, the Communists who took over Russia created the insignia to represent their party. The hammer stands for the industrial workers, and the sickle for agricultural workers. They put them together to represent their unity in supporting the Communist Party and their solidarity in protecting the communist system. It represents them working together to build their country. It's supposed to represent equality, but the Communist government oppresses the people and takes their freedom. Then they all work for the government for the same wages."

"I hope it's better in the West," Halinka sighed.

With a sharp blow of its horn, the train lurched forward. Halinka wriggled on the bench amongst her family's belongings to find a more comfortable position. Leaning close to the window, she caught a last glimpse of the train station as it disappeared in the distance.

"We are being taken to Biala Podlaska (pronounced Bee-ow-u Pod-lusku, meaning "White Forest"). It is over a hundred kilometres from here," Tata informed her. "Sleep while you can. Who knows what lies ahead?"

He nudged the picnic basket nearer to Halinka, who scooped it up in her arms and closed her eyes. For now, she would sleep, but it would not be long before she would see soldiers in different uniforms.

Chapter Twelve
THE NEW BORDER

"Wake up, Halinka!" Therese gently shook Halinka's shoulder.

"Where are we?" Halinka felt as though she had hardly slept. Each time the train had stopped, she'd awakened.

"We're in White Forest," said Therese. "People are getting off the train."

"Let's go, children," ordered Mama. "Stay close and follow Tata."

Halinka grabbed her pillow, stepped over people's belongings, and got in line behind Therese. Once off the train, they were escorted to a nearby gate and met by German soldiers, who demanded their papers. Halinka noticed that their uniforms differed from those of the Russians. They were grey-green in colour with dark green collars and shoulder straps.

"Follow me," demanded one of the guards, who led them out a rear exit. He pointed to a truck. "Climb on board and wait." Then he disappeared back into the station. The harsh sound of his voice frightened Halinka. She wasn't used to the guttural German dialect.

When they reached the truck, Tata, who had been carrying Paul, handed him to Mama. "Anne, come here," he said. "I'll give you a boost so you can help the others climb up. Therese, when you get on, Mama will pass Paul to you."

Although the truck was already overcrowded, they managed to squeeze themselves in. The fear and worry etched on people's faces mirrored Halinka's own feelings. Leaving their homes under such conditions was not only despairing, but frightening. She wondered who and what they had left behind. *What about cousin Zigmund, Auntie, Irka, and Rex? What was happening to them?* She quietly prayed for their safety.

With a roar, the truck engine started, doors slammed shut, and they began moving. Tears filled her eyes.

"Are you okay?" asked Therese, wrapping her arms around Halinka.

"I'm fine, I guess. I'm just missing everyone back home, and I hope they are all safe and that we can see them again."

"I know how you feel, Halinka. I am so grateful that at least our family is together."

Slowly, people began making conversation.

"Does anyone know where they are taking us?" asked an elderly Polish woman.

"I don't know," answered a man with a strong German accent, "but the Germans have a system in place. All we can do is wait and see what they have in mind."

Halinka could hear both Polish and German accents. She gasped, realizing that many Germans who had been living abroad were returning to their homeland. She was beginning to feel more like a true foreigner. Suddenly, little Paul's cry caught her attention, and she watched as Anne handed him to Mama.

"Halinka, could you get a small crust of bread for Paul?" Mama asked.

Halinka looked down on her lap and then frantically all around her seat. "Oh no! Where is it?" she exclaimed, her heart pounding. "I lost it!" She began to cry as a feeling of shame washed over her.

Everyone sat staring at her in disbelief. Their food—gone!

"I'm so ... sorry," Halinka stammered between sobs, tears running down her face. "I must have left it on the train!"

Tata calmly reached into a satchel by his side and pulled out a small crust of hardened bread. He passed it to Mama.

"Halinka, stop your tears. You only had a portion of the food. I have the rest. See?" He opened the satchel and revealed dried sausage, smoked pork, a loaf of bread, and cheese. "All is not lost. It was a mistake, and under the circumstances, perfectly understandable. Perhaps Mama and I are also at fault. We should have been watching more closely."

"Please don't cry, little sister," said Anne. "No one is angry."

"That's right," agreed Mama, concealing her disappointment. "Who knows, perhaps whoever finds the food will need it more than us."

Tata pulled out some dried bread and broke off pieces for each of them. He then produced a thermos full of tea mixed with lemon and honey. Since there were no cups, it was passed around so each could take a sip. The drink helped them to swallow the dry, crusty bread.

The family's words of encouragement helped Halinka feel much better. The loss of the basket had turned into a special moment for her. Even though she had made a big mistake, her family still loved and accepted her. It was one thing to be loved and accepted by your family, but she wondered how well they would be accepted in Germany.

Chapter Thirteen
FIRST CAMP

It was a short drive to their destination. Checking his pocket watch, Tata announced the journey had taken them just over an hour.

The truck's tailgate opened and they were ordered to get out. Immediately, Halinka saw the large gates they had just entered start to close. They were told to form two lines—one for the men, and the other for the women and children. Tata gave each of them a reassuring hug and whispered, "I love you."

As the men were led away, a female approached Mama and asked her to point out her children. A nearby lady saw the puzzled look on Mama's face.

"They are taking us to our barracks," she explained. "Men and women are to have separate sleeping quarters. Do not worry. We are not prisoners of war here, so you will see him later." Her soft-spoken words and smile brought comfort to Mama.

They followed the lady through the camp, which gave them an opportunity to take in their surroundings.

They passed a number of buildings, and Halinka noticed a tall, wooden fence dividing the camp. Coils of sharp barbed wire ran along the top. The fence reminded her that they were totally closed in. Perhaps they weren't prisoners of war here, but they were prisoners of their circumstances, and it frightened her. *I don't like it here. What will happen to us?*

She saw a few wooden buildings up ahead, and she watched as groups of women and children were taken inside. Finally, they stopped in front of one.

"This will be where you stay," the woman announced.

Mama led the way and slowly opened the door. A long aisle stretched to the other end of the building. On either side of the aisle were rows of wooden slatted bunkbeds; each was covered with a thin layer of straw. The small windows in the barracks allowed for little natural light, and a musty, dank odour hung heavy in the air. They had just gathered inside the doorway when Paul gave a loud cry.

Mama checked his diaper. "Anne, could you please get me a clean diaper. Jean, could you please spread a blanket on one of the beds so I can change him."

Mama was about to lay Paul down when she suddenly recoiled and gasped. "Oh no!" Seemingly out of nowhere, the blanket was covered with bugs and lice. The straw-covered beds had become their breeding ground. With her free hand, she grabbed the blanket. "There will be no sleeping on these beds tonight! Come with me. Bring everything with you."

Once outside, she handed Paul to Jean and began shaking the blanket violently. Satisfied there were no more bugs, she laid it out on the grass and proceeded to change the diaper.

"Girls, we will spend the night outside," Mama exclaimed. "Let's find a dry place that will also give some shelter from the wind."

After walking a short distance, Halinka pointed to an area between the barracks. "Look, Mama, these buildings should block the wind."

"That's very observant of you, Halinka. All right, everyone, let's go over there. Spread out some blankets and get settled."

Suddenly, Halinka saw something move out of the corner of her eye. "Tata!" she shouted.

Tata was walking briskly toward them with a smile that lit up his face. "I'm glad I found you so soon," he said as everyone swarmed around him. "How do your barracks look?"

Mama signaled for everyone to sit down. "The barracks are fine except for the bugs. We brought the blankets outside to shake them off. It'll be best to sleep outside tonight."

"Good idea," agreed Tata. "Tomorrow we will see what we can do to get rid of the bugs."

By late morning, the sun was high in the clear blue sky. It was becoming an exceptionally warm spring day.

"I'm so thirsty," sighed Therese.

"Me too," agreed Halinka.

"Ludwig, would you find out where we can get some water?" asked Mama. "The girls need a drink."

"Sure, I'll do that right now," he answered.

"Can Therese and I go too?" asked Halinka.

"Of course," replied Mama, "but ..." She hesitated, waiting for their full attention. "Do not drink out of any common cup. Rinse your hands first, and use them like this." She formed her hands into the shape of a bowl and pretended to drink. Mama was only too familiar with how easily diseases can be spread. She and Tata had been in their teens when a deadly flu infected much of Poland, Europe, and other parts of the world. Many of her relatives and neighbours had succumbed to the disease.[16]

"We will, Mama," said Therese.

---

[16] The epidemic, commonly called "The Spanish Flu," affected many countries around the world. It's estimated that it killed about fifty million people between 1918 and 1920. "The Spanish Flu," *History*, accessed January 21, 2020, history.com/topics/world-war-i/1918-flu-pandemic.

"We'll only use our hands ... after we clean them," added Halinka.

"Good."

Halinka and Therese walked arm in arm as they followed Tata. They wove in and out of small crowds of people who were also taking advantage of the warm, sunny day. Some sat on suitcases while others huddled together in quiet conversations. Young boys and girls kept themselves occupied by drawing pictures in sandy areas or playing games with strips of yarn. One young girl, around twelve years of age, glanced over and smiled at Halinka. Halinka politely returned the smile but wondered, *What in the world is there to smile about*?

Soon Tata and the two girls found a water pump beside a small shed. After carefully washing their hands, they took turns pumping the handle and drinking like Mama had shown them.

As they made their way back, the young girl approached Halinka and Therese. She introduced herself as Helga.

"Hello, my name is Halinka."

"And I'm Therese."

"And I'm Ludwig," added Tata. "Are you here with your family?"

"Yes, my parents are somewhere around here, but I like being independent," Helga replied smugly.

"It's very nice to meet you," stated Halinka, "but we must be going now." She noticed Tata waving them to move on. Although Helga seemed like a nice girl, soon the girls would discover how dangerous their friendship with her would be.

Chapter Fourteen
A CLOSE CALL

The sound of an approaching truck drew their attention to the main gates, and dust billowed high in the air as the vehicle came to a stop. The gates were opened, and a truck slowly drove to the centre of the camp. Two soldiers climbed out from the back, lowered a wooden wagon, and then placed a large pot on it. As they wheeled it into the middle of the yard, an announcement came over a loudspeaker in German. Tata listened intently.

"We must have tickets to eat," he explained when the voice stopped. "Come, let's get the rest of the family."

On the way, they met Mama and the others coming toward them.

"Girls, we have been told there is food available and that we are to line up for tickets," Mama instructed.

How does Mama know? Tata was glad someone had interpreted for Mama.

The children joined a long line of people waiting for food tickets. Then they proceeded to another line-up in front of the wagon.

The wait seemed to take forever, but finally it was Halinka's turn. She was handed a small tin bowl and a spoon. As she held out the bowl, she received a ladle full of what looked like watered-down oatmeal.

"*Danke sehr*," said Halinka. The guard nodded his head as if to show his appreciation for her use of the German language to say "thank you." She stepped aside and waited for the others.

Once everyone was served, Tata led them back to the blankets. He motioned for everyone to sit down and then gave a short prayer of thanks.

As Halinka scooped up her last bite, she sighed. "Therese, I think I could have eaten three of these."

"Me too!" agreed Therese.

Just then, baby Paul began to cry. He had been crying a lot lately; everyone knew it was due to hunger.

"Hush," said Mama softly, feeling helpless as she held him in her arms.

"I have an idea!" said Halinka, standing up. (She hated to see her little brother crying from hunger.) "I'm going to ask the guard for another bowl."

Too shocked to say anything, Jean and Anne could only gasp as they watched Halinka walk toward the guard manning the large pot. Each person was only allowed one bowl.

"She looks like David going to meet Goliath!" exclaimed Therese, remembering the Bible story of how young David faced the giant.

Mama and Tata had to agree. With the surly-looking guard at least two metres tall, and Halinka just over one metre, it was quite an intimidating sight.

The closer Halinka got, the bigger he appeared, and the more scared she felt. *Can I really do this? Surely God will give me the courage I need.*

"*Bitte mehr* (More please)." Her voice quivered as she held out the bowl.

"Nein!" The guard gruffly waved her away.

She knew that meant no, but she decided to stand her ground. Mustering up her courage once again, she asked, "*Bitte mehr?*"

He stared down at her intently and then grabbed the ladle, scooped some up, and dropped it into her bowl.

"*Vielen dank* (Thank you very much)," she said with a smile. She then quickly turned and hurried back to the others, in case he changed his mind.

"Mama, look!" She held out the bowl.

"Thank you, Halinka. How in the world did you manage to get another bowl?" Mama asked, bewildered.

Hearing the question, Jean spoke up. "That girl? She always seems to find a way!" They all laughed.

Halinka spoon-fed Paul, and it wasn't long before he was smiling and cooing happily.

After all the bowls and utensils were returned, the truck was loaded up and driven away. They spent the rest of the afternoon exploring the camp to find the outhouses and where people could clean up. Halinka and Therese played some games with Helen as they took her for a short walk.

"Halinka! Therese!"

The girls turned toward the direction of the voice. It belonged to Helga.

"Come here," she admonished in a hushed tone, waving frantically for them to join her between two of the barracks.

The girls glanced side to side with uncertainty and then took Helen by the hand and approached Helga. Helga smiled brightly as she led them to the back of the barracks and pointed. Halinka gasped. Beside Helga's crumpled winter coat lay a small, square, wooden apparatus with a circular speaker grille in the middle of it. Underneath were two knobs and a tuning dial. Halinka and Therese recognized it immediately. It was a shortwave radio!

"Where ... where did you get that?" Therese asked.

"My dad purchased it in Germany a few years back but got rid of it, or so he thought, when the Nazis made it illegal to own them. This one is called the Deutscher Kleinempffanger DK38," Helga explained, proud of her knowledge. "I saw where he disposed of it and I've had it ever since. It's really known as 'Goebbel's Snout' because of its small size," she added boastfully.

In 1933, Joseph Goebbels, the Minister of Propaganda, had seen the great propaganda potential of the shortwave radio. He'd made it readily affordable so that all of Germany could hear the voice of the Fuhrer, Hitler himself. The DKE 38 shortwave radio lacked shortwave bands, but it was good enough for everyone to hear the Nazi messages from within Germany. However, people soon realized that with an external antenna, they could receive foreign stations after dark. Also, stations such as the BBC European service increased their transmission power as the war progressed, making them more easily attainable. When the war began, it became a criminal offence in Nazi Germany to listen to foreign stations. In occupied Poland, non-German citizens were not allowed to listen to the radio at all.

During the war, people secretly listened to the London, England broadcasts. Many of the radio transmitters had been destroyed in Eastern and Western Europe by the Nazis, except for those in London. This made it impossible for the Nazis to know what every household was listening to, so they made it a treasonable offense to listen to overseas broadcasts. About 1,500 Germans were imprisoned in the first year of the war for listening to London-based broadcasts. However, listening to broadcasts from other countries was very popular during the war, even though it was illegal.

The Minister of the Interior and the creator of the Reich Broadcasting Corporation, Erich Scholz, declared, "The German radio serves the German people. That which degraded the German people is excluded from German radio."[17]

"Watch this." Helga crouched down and adjusted the coil wire antenna. "After dark, when the antenna is extended, it picks up stations from other countries. She nervously glanced around the corner.

"*Fraulines!*" A German guard had spotted them and was quickly strutting toward them.

Halinka instinctively grabbed a nearby twig and began drawing in the dirt, while Helga quickly threw her coat over the radio and leaned back, pressing against it.

"Here, Therese, your turn! You draw the next line," Halinka nervously shouted.

---

17 Glenn Aylett, "Hitler's Radio," *Transdiffusion Broadcasting System*, (accessed December 27, 2019), https://www.transdiffusion.org/2008/01/07/hitlers_radio.

Therese grasped the twig from Halinka's outstretched hand and drew an adjoining line. Suddenly, little Helen became frightened, let out a scream, and clung to Halinka's arm.

"Come, Helen, draw a line with me," Halinka encouraged, distracting as much attention away from Helga as possible. The guard stopped in front of them. Helga was quietly sitting on the ground and looking as though she hadn't a care in the world.

"What are you doing here?" the guard clamored.

"We are taking turns ... and ... and playing a drawing game," Halinka blurted out. She handed the stick back to Therese.

"You are not allowed back here. *Bewegen* (pronounced beveegan, meaning 'move')," ordered the guard.

As Helga slowly arose, Halinka dared not look at her. She quickly marched away with Therese and little Helen, anger burning inside her. *What if ... if ... we were all caught with that radio?* She shuddered at the thought. Helga was too much of a risk-taker!

After the guard departed, Helga caught up to them. "Whew! That was close," she whispered, clasping the hidden radio concealed in her coat.

"Helga, that was too dangerous! You should never have brought a radio into this camp," Halinka scolded.

"Let alone listen to broadcasts from outside of Germany. That's illegal."

Halinka determined from that moment on to stay clear of Helga.

"Come, Therese, Helen. Let's find Tata." She couldn't wait to tell him.

When they found him, the girls told Tata about their involvement with Helga and the close call with the guard.

"I am so glad you didn't get caught. It's best to stay away from her for now. I'll speak with her and try to persuade her to leave that radio alone. She reminds me a bit of your Uncle Ernest." Tata shook his head. Halinka's face lit up at the mention of his name.

"Tata, did Uncle Ernest ever get rid of his radio?" Halinka loved her uncle and had many fond memories of his visits, especially of the times he took them for carriage rides around the town and bought them candy.

"I don't know if he ever got rid of it, but I do hope he never gets caught!" Worry etched Halinka's brow. Thoughts of Uncle Ernest and his radio continually plagued Halinka's mind throughout the war.

Later, as it grew dark, a heavy weariness settled on everyone. The main yard emptied quickly as people left to find their place for the night. Mama and Tata led the family to where they would spend the first night sleeping outside. Once they settled down, Tata prayed with them before leaving for the men's barracks. It was a great comfort to see their father's faith in God, even when times were so bad.

Halinka laid quietly, the blanket softly draped over her. The hard, uneven ground poking into her side was of no comfort. She recalled the Old Testament Bible story of Jacob sleeping outside and using a stone for his pillow. How uncomfortable that must have been! *At least I have a pillow!* She smiled and then snuggled into her pillow's softness.

Suddenly, the distant sound of a dog barking permeated Halinka's thoughts and reminded her of Rex. Tears trickled down her cheeks as she silently prayed for his safety.

Chapter Fifteen
THE SONG

In the dim light of the pre-dawn sky, Halinka awoke with a start. The sound of men's melodic voices rose high in the air.

"Therese," she whispered, "do you hear that?"

Therese opened her eyes. "What? Is it really singing?"

"Yes," answered Halinka. "It woke me up." She pointed to a section of the wooden fence dividing the camp. "I think it's coming from over there."

"Let's take a look," suggested Therese, gently removing her blanket. Quietly, they crept to the fence, hoping to see through to the other side.

Their search ended soon as Therese whispered, "Halinka, over here! I found a small hole."

Halinka scurried over, bent down, and peered through the opening. A large group of Polish male prisoners were singing a well-known patriotic love song. Arm in arm they stood, voices blending harmoniously. A wave of pride welled up within Halinka.

The sight of her fellow countrymen singing so passionately would be forever etched in Halinka's heart and mind. Therese, too, stood in awe as she peered through the hole and listened to the song.

> The buds of white roses flowered,
> Come back, Johnny, from this war!
> Back and kiss like the years before;
> I'll give you for this, the most beautiful rose!
> When you were going to war,
> I put the white rose on your rifle.
> What would I give you now, Johnny?
> Hey, if you come back to your girlfriend from the war.
> Hey, girl, a cavalry man died in the fight,
> Even though you gave him the white rose.
> War is insincere to the gift of your hands,
> Or maybe the passion of your heart went out.
> Johnny doesn't need anything right now.
> The buds of white roses are already flowered for him.

There, under the ravine, where he died,
The white roses have grown on the grave.[18]

Help us all, Lord, to make it, Halinka prayed, her face now wet with tears. The fate of these prisoners was never known to Halinka. Were they shot? Were they transported to another prison? Did some escape?

---

18 "White Roses," also known as "Blossomed Buds of White Roses," is a Polish military and patriotic song created around 1918 and composed by Mieczyslaw Kozar-Słobódzkiego. The song was a reminder of families torn apart, of the hurt, pain, and death brought on by war.

Chapter Sixteen
THE BUGS

A voice came over the camp loudspeakers. Morning rations had arrived. Within minutes, the whole camp came alive as people made their way to the truck. This daily routine was as predictable as the rising sun. Three meals were served each day. Breakfast consisted of a watered-down oatmeal; for lunch they were given a thin soup with a piece of hard bread, and for supper they ate a bland stew.

After the radio incident, Halinka and Therese only saw Helga from a distance. True to his word, Tata had spoken to Helga; however, he was uncertain she would heed his advice. Once, Halinka saw Helga slip behind the barracks. *Has she been listening to the radio again?* Halinka couldn't help but fear for Helga's safety, and Uncle Ernest's too ...if he still had a radio.

Later that week, a cold north wind blew in and caused the temperature to plummet. After supper that evening, Mama reluctantly announced that they would have to sleep inside the barracks. It was inevitable. They would have to deal with the bugs.

"I've been thinking, Therese," said Halinka as she stood and looked at her bed, "if we fold our blankets in half, we can get in between them and hopefully keep some of the bugs away."

"Good idea," agreed Therese. "Let's try it!"

As they folded their blankets, Halinka continued. "God made all the bugs, didn't He?"

"Of course," laughed Therese, wondering where this question was leading.

"Then we should thank Him and welcome them as our friends."

Therese laughed. "That's absurd, Halinka!"

Later, in the darkness, Halinka began to feel the slight movement of bugs on her head. Panic gripped her heart, so she began to whisper over and over, "Thank you, God, for all these bugs." She finally drifted into a fitful sleep.

There was definitely a lice epidemic, and by week's end, raw and bleeding scalps were seen throughout the camp with no relief in sight.

"My head hurts, Halinka," whimpered Helen.

"Mine does too, but things will get better. You wait and see."

At that moment, an announcement came over the camp's loudspeakers.

The Bugs

"Attention. At nine o'clock tomorrow morning, everyone will be transported to another camp. Be ready."

"Tata, where are they taking us now?" Halinka asked.

"Further west," he replied. "We're still in Poland, in the territory now called New Germany."

"I hope the next camp is better," exclaimed Halinka, "with no bugs or lice!"

Tata sighed. "Let us hope and pray that it's not any worse."

To cope with the lice, the girls had decided earlier that week to give some of them names.

"I think John, Peter, and Alina are visiting my head tonight. What about you?" asked Halinka, scratching her head as she lay in bed.

"I'm sure it's Christopher, Stella, and Leopold visiting me," replied Therese. The girls giggled in spite of their terrible circumstances.

"Hush up, girls, it's time to sleep," admonished Mama. "We do not know what tomorrow will bring." It was good Mama didn't know, for terror would have gripped her heart.

Chapter Seventeen
THE SHOWER

The next morning after breakfast, the camp was a hive of activity as people gathered up their meagre belongings. What they couldn't carry in their hands they once again strapped to their bodies.

Soon the sound of a truck convoy was heard coming through the main gates.

"Hurry," ordered Tata, "and be ready. We are leaving shortly."

When finished, they waited outside while Tata made one last check. Halinka's earlier loss of the food basket prompted him to make sure nothing was left behind.

As they reached the truck, they saw that people were already lined up and boarding. It was a drab and dismal sight. With nowhere to wash clothing, and limited resources for personal hygiene, they looked like an unkempt and beggarly lot.

Soon everyone was loaded and a signal given to depart. For two long hours they were jostled about

The Shower

until, finally, the trucks came to a halt. The new camp was different in that it only had a small compound and a single building. The tailgates were flung open and a command given to disembark. Tata jumped down first to help the others. Everyone stood and waited to see what would happen next.

Instructions were broadcast in German, so Tata translated to Mama. "I am to go to the left with the men. You and the children are to go over there," he pointed. "They want us to go through some showers." Tata quickly kissed Mama and went to join the other men.

Mama looked alarmed. A strong and peculiar odour emanated from the building. It reminded her of bitter almonds.

"What's that odour, Mama?" asked Anne.

"I don't know, but I smell it too," she answered anxiously.

As she looked ahead through the throng of women and children, Halinka could see a long brick building with two doors divided by a partition. The men were being directed through one, and a female guard was directing women and children through the other. People around her were whispering.

"What kind of shower is this?" asked a woman.

"Is it one of those gas chambers we've been hearing about?" asked a young, distraught mother.

"I don't know," quivered another voice.

Gas chamber? Halinka's heart pounded. *What is that?* She looked at Therese. "What is a gas chamber?"

"I don't know," answered Therese anxiously, her voice quivering.

As they inched forward, Halinka and the others soon found themselves next to enter.

"Mama, what's happening?" she asked.

Before Mama could answer, a scream was heard from within. "No! No!" a woman screeched.

"I don't know, Halinka," replied Mama, putting her arm around her shoulder, "but let us hope it is not bad for us." Mama was really trying to convince herself.

At the entrance, they were instructed to go into the dimly lit room, remove their clothing, place it on a moving conveyor belt, and walk toward a distant light.

Mama froze. "No! I have heard about these extermination camps where they gas people to death. You are going to kill us!" Halinka had never seen Mama so terrified!

"Keep moving! You are being deloused." The angry guard shoved Mama ahead.

"Come, children." Mama, knowing she had no choice, reached back to grasp Anne's hand, not knowing whether the guard was telling the truth or not.

Everyone huddled closely together as they moved forward into the dark room.

The Shower

"Okay, children, take off your clothes, place them on the conveyer belt, and walk beside them." They followed Mama's instructions.

One step! Two steps! Three steps! They had entered the next room. As they continued moving forward, shower heads above them spewed out fine streams of powdery liquid. The hissing noise made it believable ... for a few seconds .... that it was a gas. The fine mist covered their bodies, and the strong chemical odour made them feel nauseous.

"Look down. Cover ... your mouth .... and eyes," Mama stammered. "Walk quickly." She covered Paul's face with her free hand.[19]

Thankful to be alive, they reached the exit door. Once through, they went into the change rooms, got dressed, and walked outside into the sunlight.

---

[19] This "mist" was a fine, diluted spray of a gas called Zyklon-B. In minimal doses, it was effective for fumigating people, clothing, equipment, and buildings. In higher doses, it became a lethal means of eliminating people—even large groups at once. At this point in the war, the Nazis had not yet begun to use permanent buildings as gas chambers. Prior to this, as early as 1939, mobile gas units were used to kill people with mental or physical disabilities, or anyone, including their own people, whom the Nazis judged to be unfit. These mobile units were equipped with chemically manufactured carbon monoxide gas. Although the Nazis tried to keep it a secret, rumours abounded that these units did exist. Later in the war, as they built more permanent buildings, they were able to kill up to two thousand people at once. It's estimated that between 1941 and 1945, several million people of all ages lost their lives in this manner.

Although the air was cool, Halinka could feel the sun's heat penetrate deep through her damp clothing and into her body.

"There's Tata," she announced, pointing as he walked briskly toward them.

"How is everyone?" Tata asked, giving each of them a hug.

"Oh, Ludwig," cried Mama, with a look of relief on her face, "I was so worried, but we are fine."

"Tata, are the Nazis really sending people to gas chambers to get rid of them?" asked Jean.

The question caught him off guard. It was getting more difficult to shield his family from the horrors of war. He answered vaguely, "They are rounding up anyone who appears to be a threat, or who cannot or will not work for their purposes."

"Why does Hitler hate the Polish people so much?" asked Therese.

"Well," replied Tata, carefully choosing his words, "Hitler believes the Germans are the superior race. In his mind, the Polish people are the lowest class and should be either enslaved or killed. The Nazis have taken over public and private properties in Poland, and are either destroying or changing anything that doesn't fit into their plan to Germanize the country. As for the Jews, he wants to destroy them all."

"I hate the Nazis," blurted out Halinka. "I wish I didn't have any German blood in me!"

"Halinka!" whispered Tata, grabbing her firmly by the shoulders. "Don't ever talk like that. If the wrong people hear you, we will all be in danger for opposing the Nazis."

Therese nodded in sombre agreement

"Well, I hate what they are doing," exclaimed Halinka defensively, harboured hatred spurring her words. The more she found out about the Nazis, the more she despised them, her rage increasingly sharpened at the thought of so many people being mistreated and killed.

"I don't like what is happening either," agreed Tata. "Right now we're considered Germans because of our ancestry, so we must act like it."

"Come," a guard bellowed, and soon the trucks were on their way.

Although no one knew it yet, their next destination would be Pabianice, a community still within the old Polish border.

Chapter Eighteen
PABIANICE

The roads through this part of the countryside were better, making the ride more tolerable than the previous one. Halinka pulled back part of the canopy at the rear of the truck to view the serene, flat land that was covered in patches of daisy-like flowers, shrubs, and small trees. Poland was a land of diverse terrain with hot, dry, sandy areas, high mountain ranges, fertile plains, swamps, extensive forests with many lakes, and some large rivers. Halinka could also see army trucks, soldiers with guns, and tanks crawling everywhere. War! The natural beauty of the landscape stood in stark contrast to the harsh realities of life brought on by this war.

As the family continued westward, large fields and farmland filled the landscape. A few hours later, they entered a more densely populated area. The trucks slowed, turned off the main road, and soon stopped in front of a large wrought iron gate. Soldiers lifted the truck canopies and ordered everyone out. They passed single file through the gate into a large courtyard.

"I overheard the guards talking," Tata whispered to Mama. "They want to check everyone's papers here and then relocate us."

"*Nicht sprechen!* (No talking)," a guard shrieked. Tata immediately stopped.

Soon they entered a large office filled with desks, military officers, and secretaries. To the right was a staircase leading up to the next floor.

"Follow me," the guard motioned. Tata led the way up the stairs, walking behind the guard. At the top, the guard walked to a door on the left, pointed for them to enter, then returned downstairs.

The room they entered was empty except for a pile of mattresses off to one side.

"Bring your belongings over here," Tata said, placing his satchel on the floor. "This will be our area."

Immediately another family walked through the door. In total, seventeen people crowded together to make this room their temporary home.

"Mama, can we take off our outer clothes now?" asked Halinka. Sweat dripped down her forehead as the rising heat from the outside filled the upstairs room.

"Certainly," replied Mama. She looked at Jean. "Could you please help the girls take off their extra clothes, fold them, and put them in our corner?"

"Yes, Mama," responded Jean.

They were relieved to remove their dirty outer clothing, not only because of the heat, but especially since they had not been able to wash anything for at least two weeks. Suddenly, Paul began to cry from hunger.

"We must all eat," exclaimed Tata. It was now mid-afternoon.

Tata instructed everyone to sit on the floor in a tight circle. Then he reached into his satchel and pulled out a dried pork sausage.

"Where did you get that?" gasped Anne.

Halinka clasped her hands together in delight, and before she could speak, Tata put a finger to his mouth.

"We must keep this to ourselves," he whispered. "Food is scarce, and if others find out we have some, they may try to take what little we have left." He divided the sausage into small pieces and discreetly distributed them amongst the family.

"This is so good, Tata," said Halinka, savouring every bite.

"Yes, Tata, thank you," added Therese.

His face lit up with a smile. Providing for his family meant a lot to him, even if there wasn't much he could offer.

"Tata, can Therese and I go exploring?" asked Halinka when she had finished her last bite.

Therese stared at her, wide-eyed.

"Yes," he replied, in a tone that reminded the girls of the need for caution. *Listen a lot, say little*, Tata had told them before. Neither girl wanted to get their family in trouble.

From the upstairs hallway window, Therese and Halinka could see the street below. It was neatly lined with small shops and office buildings.

"Come on," exclaimed Halinka with a wave of her hand, "let's go."

She led the way toward the stairs. At the bottom, a German guard noticed them.

"Halt," he ordered, and then pointed at a small side door to indicate where they were allowed to go.

"*Danke*," answered the girls, forcing themselves to smile. They quickly bolted out the door.

"I really don't care for all these guards everywhere. I'm glad we're finally alone out here," Therese sighed with relief.

"Me too!" exclaimed Halinka. "I feel like we're in a fish bowl with all these soldiers and guards glaring at us! Magnifying glass, anyone?" The girls snickered together.

The small enclosed back yard, bare earth, small patches of neglected, yellowish-green grass, and one lone shrub in a far corner welcomed them.

"What a sad and lonely sight," remarked Therese. "I wonder how long we'll be at this place."

"I wish I knew," Halinka sighed. "Let's go back upstairs. There's nothing here."

As the girls turned to leave, the door suddenly swung open, and out stepped Helga.

"Hello, Halinka. Hello, Therese." Her face flushed with embarrassment.

"Hi, Helga," the girls replied. Awkwardness hung in the air.

"Do ... do you want to play a game?" Helga asked. The look on her face indicated that she yearned for companionship. From inside her pocket, Helga pulled out a skipping rope.

"Wow," exclaimed Halinka. "I haven't skipped since we were in school back home."

The girls were so ecstatic, they offered to turn the rope so Helga could jump first. It felt good to play and have fun, all thanks to Helga. Perhaps Helga wasn't so bad after all.

A little while later, after returning upstairs, everyone was directed to a room where they would receive a small portion of pork and potatoes. After the meal, they returned to their quarters and prepared for bed. Mattresses were laid out in clusters as families gathered together for their evening rest. Two meals a day and very little to do would be their monotonous routine until they departed.

Since leaving home, Halinka and her family had encountered German guards and soldiers, but not members of Hitler's notorious Nazi Party. This, however, was soon to change.

Chapter Nineteen
SUMMONED

"Therese, come quickly," Halinka whispered early one morning, so as not to awaken anyone else. She stood quietly by the bedroom window.

Therese scampered softly across the floor and peered out onto the dimly lit street. Three cars had pulled up and stopped below them. They watched as half a dozen soldiers in Nazi uniforms got out of the cars. On their left arms were distinct red bands, each with a white circle and a black, peculiar-shaped symbol inside of it. It was the first time Halinka had ever seen the symbol called a "swastika."[20]

"Why are they here?" Therese gasped, watching them enter the building.

---

20 The swastika's use by the Nazis was linked to the belief that the German people were descendants of the Aryan race. They used it as a symbol of good fortune and prosperity. The Nazis considered the early Aryans to be the supreme example of white invaders, so they incorporated the symbol as their own. To the Nazis, it represented the strength and greatness of Germany.

"I don't know," answered Halinka, "but we should tell Mama and Tata."

"What is it girls?" Tata had overheard them and came to see what was happening.

"We just saw Nazi soldiers come into the building," answered Therese anxiously.

"They must be here to check papers," Tata explained. "I overheard one of the guards yesterday say they would be looking for criminals and forged papers, but they never said how soon."

"We will be okay, won't we?" asked Halinka nervously.

"Yes, don't worry. We've passed every inspection so far." Tata wrapped his arms around her.[21]

Throughout the morning, soldiers came and went, ushering people to and from their interrogations. It was now early afternoon.

"Kutsche," a soldier bellowed.

"*Ja, ich bin hier* (I am here)," replied Tata. Halinka found it strange to hear him speak German so often now. She needed to understand and speak it better

---

21 When the Russians opened the borders for people to leave, they took advantage of the situation to get rid of undesirables, such as known criminals and trouble makers. These people were intentionally released from prisons to be sent to Germany. That way, the Russians didn't have to deal with them. Also, many Jews, freedom fighters, and spies carried forged passports and other documents to avoid capture by the Nazis.

herself! Learning the German language would help her disguise her Polish identity.

With papers in hand, Tata followed the guard downstairs.

Back upstairs, Mama looked worried. "Children," she called, "please pray for your father, that the Lord will continue to give him favour, wisdom, and strength." Halinka noticed tears crystalizing in Mama's eyes. Jean reached over and hugged her.

Mama knew that their fate was in the hands of the governing Nazis. Every citizen residing in Poland of German descent had been placed on the "German People's List" (*Deutsche Volkliste*) and divided into four categories. They ranged from those who identified themselves as German, to Poles who may be considered capable of Germanization.

Tata and Mama fell into the category that included people who were ethnic Germans but Polonized, like Tata. The hope was that these people could be won back to Germany. It also included non-Germans, like Mama, who were married to Germans. Everyone in this group acquired German citizenship, but it was subject to revocation. Any hint of disloyalty to the German cause would be considered treason, and the outcome would be unfavourable. Conviction of such an offense would mean either being sent to a concentration camp or killed.

Downstairs, Tata disappeared into one of the offices, a den full of Nazis. The door closed behind him as he entered.

After Halinka's prayer for Tata, she could no longer sit still. "Mama, Therese and I will go downstairs and wait for Tata ... if we may?"

"I will allow it," Mama replied.

"We'll stay here," Anne stated, squeezing Mama's hand reassuringly.

The girls quickly scurried down and perched themselves on a nearby bench. They watched anxiously as men and women in Nazi uniforms bustled about in a frenzy.

Suddenly, an office door opened and a frightened gentleman was roughly escorted out by soldiers.

Were his papers forged? Was he a criminal from Russia, or did he display any hint of resistance to Germanization? Halinka's thoughts swirled with possible reasons for his revocation. She turned away, for it was too distressing to watch the helpless, unprotected man. Therese and Halinka locked eyes. Each girl could see her own fear and concern for Tata reflected in the other's eyes.

Another door opened, and the girls could see Tata! He was facing an officer and standing by a desk. The officer raised his hand and saluted. "Heil Hitler."

To the girls' amazement, Tata returned the same salute. "Heil Hitler."

"Welcome to the Third Reich!" The Nazi smiled.

The Third Reich referred to Nazi Germany. They were being welcomed into the "German Empire," with Hitler as their dictator. Halinka inwardly shuddered at the thought. *The Third Reich? Salute Hitler? How could Tata do such a thing?*

"Let's go back upstairs," he announced, approaching the girls with a look of relief. "Mama will be relieved to hear that we've been accepted into Germany."

Mama was indeed relieved, and she cried while Tata embraced her. Her tears were bittersweet, though, because acceptance into the Third Reich meant renouncing Poland and joining the enemy. But so far, they were escaping death!

Later that evening when Tata and Halinka were alone, she asked him why he had saluted and said "Heil Hitler."

"Halinka," he answered, "I am not able to join any army because of my leg, my disability, so I have to do what I can to keep our family safe. We must come to Germany; otherwise, it will be death for all of us!"

"But," Halinka whispered, "I thought they were our enemies, like the Russians, and that we don't believe in what Hitler is doing."

Tata gently took her chin in his hand so that she would look into his eyes. "You are right, but what do you think would have happened if I refused to return the salute, or showed any resistance?"

She thought for a moment. "They may have locked you up or killed you."

"Worse," he agreed. "They would have separated all of us and put us into concentration camps. Remember, they have the power to revoke our citizenship if they question our loyalty to them. We would lose our status and protection."

Halinka gasped, vividly remembering the man downstairs who was taken away.

She also remembered that Tata knew what the Nazis planned for the Polish people. In 1939, he had heard Hitler's Obersalzberg speech: "The Poles ... I have placed my death head formation in readiness—for the present only in the east—with orders to [his army] to send to death mercilessly and without compassion, men, women, and children, of Polish derivation and language ..."[22]*

"Oh Tata," she cried, wrapping her arms around his neck. "I do trust you."

That trust would soon be tested when they learned the true cost of their acceptance into the Third Reich.

---

22 *Wikipedia, The Free Encyclopedia,* s.v. "Hitler's Obersalzberg Speech,"(accessed December 27, 2019), https://en.wikipedia.org/wiki/Hitler%27s_Obersalzberg_Speech#German_and_English_wording.

Chapter Twenty
THE SEARCH

At the end of August 1940, within a few weeks of the Kutsche family's acceptance into the Third Reich, the family was taken by truck and then train westward into Germany, Hitler's Fatherland. Eventually, they arrived at the town of Gieboldehausen, meaning "Golden House." From there they were driven to a work camp outside of town, where once again they were fenced in. The camp was surrounded by low-lying hills that were dotted with forests and blanketed with various field crops.

"Let's put our stuff over here." Halinka wearily dragged her belongings about ten paces away from the truck. Therese followed and dropped hers next to Halinka's.

"Therese! Halinka!" Helga jumped off the next truck and ran toward them. Halinka noticed how gently she placed her belongings on the ground.

"I am so tired and hungry," Helga sighed. "I wonder ..."

The Search

"*Frauline!*" a guard spoke raucously. "Come back! We have orders to check everyone's belongings from your truck. Bring your things here!"

Helga froze. Alarmed, Halinka realized what was in Helga's possession.

Helga was in a precarious state. She and her family had been accepted as German citizens, but their position was vulnerable. Their family's loyalty to the German Reich could be in question should Helga be found with a radio. She had taken too big of a risk.

"Leave it," Halinka breathed, not daring to move her lips. Helga quickly scooped up all but one of her belongings and ran toward the guard. The pillow with the forbidden secret lay just to the left of Halinka.

"Halinka!" gasped Therese. "What are you doing?"

"We must help Helga. Come quickly; let's find Tata and Mama," Halinka whispered.

Therese grabbed Halinka's pillow with her own belongings, leaving room for Halinka to carry Helga's.

"Thanks." Halinka bent down and carefully tucked the lone pillow in behind her blanket.

"*Offnen* (Open)!" They could hear a guard in the distance demanding that someone open their bag. The girls hurried to find Tata.

"The women have just been asked to meet at the housing complex over there. Hurry, girls," Tata whispered, pointing to the right.

The girls saw Mama and followed her inside. Their living quarters was a small room lined with straw-filled mattresses. At this camp, they would be the sole occupants of the room. Halinka and Therese carefully hid Helga's pillow under their blankets.

"Girls, we're to go for a meal right now," Jean informed them. "Come with me." She affectionately took them by the arms and led them out the door. As they stepped out, Halinka was greeted by a crying Helga, who ran over and squeezed her arm.

"Thank you so much."

Before responding, Halinka turned to Jean and Therese. "You two go on ahead. I'll come with Helga in a bit."

"Don't be late. We can't get into any trouble," ordered Jean in her older sister tone.

"I won't."

With the girls out of earshot, Halinka whispered, "Helga, you must get rid of it."

"I know. I'm so sorry I put you in such danger. How do I get rid of it now?"

Halinka thought for a moment. She looked around and saw the different buildings, the garden, and the outhouses. Then an idea dawned on her. "I've got it!"

"What?" Helga asked with anticipation.

"Let's throw the radio into one of the outhouse holes."

"That's a great idea. No one will think to look down there!"

"The stench alone will keep everyone's noses and eyes away," Halinka added. "We'll have to wait until it's almost dark. Let's meet at the far outhouse just before the curfew."

"Okay," Helga agreed. "But now we need to hurry and get our food before they miss us."

After the meal and while they were getting ready for bed, Halinka knew that she must prepare for a more unpredictable and possibly hazardous task. She and her family would be in danger if the radio was discovered. Tata would be very upset with her if he knew what she was about to do. Would Helga be true to her word and meet her? Looking in the direction of the setting sun, Halinka prayed that all would go as planned.

Chapter Twenty-One
THE OUTHOUSE

Halinka stepped outside and briskly walked toward the outhouses.

"Where are you going, *Frauline*?" A lady officer stepped in behind her. Halinka froze. She dared not turn around, for fear the bulge under her coat would be noticed.

"To ... the toilet," Halinka stammered.

Satisfied with the answer, the officer stated, "Very well, but be quick about it. It is almost curfew." She then turned to go.

"*Danke.*" Halinka breathed a sigh of relief and hurried away, trembling with fear over how close she had come to being caught.

When she reached the outhouse, she slowly opened the door and peeked inside. *Where is Helga?* Helga arrived a few seconds later, but the wait had felt like an eternity to Halinka. They quickly stepped in and closed the door.

Without wasting a second, Halinka removed the radio from under her coat. Together, the girls pushed it through the toilet opening. They heard a dull splat as it landed at the bottom. It gurgled as it slowly sank into the slime.

Satisfied, Halinka turned to Helga. "We're done."

Helga, lost for words, squeezed her friend tightly in thanks then stepped outside.

Suddenly, out of nowhere, the same guard who had questioned Halinka stood before Helga.

"*Frauline*, what are you doing out here? Do you not know that it is almost curfew time?"

"I was just heading back to bed. The stars look beautiful tonight," Helga responded as calmly as possible. "I better get going now."

Still inside the outhouse, Halinka stood tensely, shocked by the sound of the guard's voice. She could hardly breathe. She listened as Helga's quick moving footsteps diminished in the distance. But where was the guard? Halinka dared not move. Did the guard know Halinka was in the stall? Thankfully, the sound of the guard's footsteps began to fade away. Slowly, she opened the creaking door, slipped out, and made her way back to her sleeping quarters.

As she walked toward the barracks, Halinka couldn't help but think of Uncle Ernest back in

Wolkowysk. Had he gotten rid of his shortwave radio? Was he being extra careful, or ... she dared not think the rest.

Chapter Twenty-Two
ALL FOR THE FATHERLAND

"Jean, what's happening?" Alarm sounded in Halinka's voice as they stood outside and took in the scene before them.

That morning, everyone had been ordered to gather outside immediately.

"I don't know. Who knows anything? Let's join the others."

Jean and Halinka quickly walked across the yard to Mama, Anne, Therese, Helen, and Paul. Among the army trucks, a group of officers and nuns mingled together like misfits of war and peace.

Tata, accompanied by an officer and nun, anxiously approached the family.

"Olga, they have asked for Jean. She must go for duty. All girls fifteen years and older are needed."

"What duty? How far away?" Mama gasped, her voice shaking with emotion. She reached for Jean's arm and held it tightly. The nun placed her hand on Mama's shoulder.

Tata interpreted as the nun spoke. "We have orders to take her. Once we get to the convent, we will determine where she is most needed. She must leave with us immediately."

"For how long?" Mama asked.

"We can't be sure. I'm sorry," the nun replied.

Taking Jean in her arms, Mama sobbed. "I love you, Jean."

Tears flowed down Jean's face as she hugged Mama back.

"I'm scared," Jean whispered. Mama drew up her shoulders and held Jean at arm's length.

"God is with you wherever you go. Remember that, no matter what." The soldier grabbed Jean's arm and ripped her away from Mama.

"Mama!" Jean cried as she disappeared into the crowd. The nun laid her hand on Mama's arm again, a tear glistening in her eye, before she turned to follow the soldier. For a moment the world stopped. Mama fell to the ground, defeated.

Halinka watched helplessly. Tata pulled Mama up into his arms, and together they wept for the loss of their daughter and the fear of what might happen to her.

Little did they know that things would get far worse before they would get better.

Early the next morning, soldiers ordered all the men into the courtyard. Once they were assembled, an officer announced, "You are needed for the cause of the Reich. You must come with us immediately."

Tata quickly ran and embraced each member of the family before making his way back to the group of men. Halinka could see the look of despair on his face. Their family was once again being manipulated by forces beyond their control.

Leaving his family at the mercy of the Nazis was breaking his heart. His only hope was that God would somehow, by a miracle, keep them safe and reunite them.

Everyone stood stunned and in a state of shock. As the weary group of men were led away, Tata turned and shouted, "Don't give up! We will be together again."

Halinka began to cry as she clasped Therese's hand. "What's happening?" she sobbed, "First Jean and now Tata."

Everyone wondered where they were taking them. They had no idea that the men's skills and experiences would determine their destinations.

Halinka watched with a saddened heart as Tata boarded one of the army trucks off in the distance.

"Tata!" she screamed, but her voice was drowned out by the loud revving of the trucks' engines as they departed. The thought of never seeing him again was unbearable, and poor Mama ... Once again, hatred for the Germans boiled up inside of her.

As the girls turned and walked away, she thought about Jean and Tata. *Will they ever be with us again?* Although she was determined to pray and even hope against all hope, could she continue to endure Hitler's Reign of Terror?

Book Three
INSIDE GERMANY

"Weeping may endure for a night, but joy comes in the morning."

—Psalm 30:5

PROLOGUE

What is endurance? Endurance is the courage to keep going in the midst of pain and hardship. The people who lived under Hitler's "Reign of Terror" understood what this meant, as they had to keep moving forward despite their misery. As the war pressed on, they suffered increasingly from hunger, cold, thirst, and constant fear.

Inside Germany, people could only hope and pray for an end to the torment. The number of Germans who were tired of the war grew steadily each day. Instead of viewing themselves as the conquerors of Europe, they saw themselves as the first victims of the Nazis. By 1943, Goebbels, the Minister of Propaganda, knew that enthusiasm was waning in Germany. Instead of appealing to the people, he used threats and punishment to motivate them into voluntary work for the government. Hitler's 300,000 SS guards and 150,000 armed police patrols and forces were being used—not to fight the enemy but to police the

Germans themselves. Hitler and the Nazis were not only fighting on three fronts—they were fighting on a fourth against their own people.[23]

---

23 Alfred Kantorowicz, "Inside Germany," *Maclean's*, August 1, 1943, 12–13.

Chapter Twenty-Three
UNEXPECTED NEWS

All the Kutsche family could do was endure. By the late fall of 1940, there was no end of war in sight. Germany had not only conquered Poland, but also Denmark, France, Belgium, Luxemburg, Norway, and the Netherlands.

The Nazis attempted to "Germanize" Poland by forcibly removing Polish citizens from their property and sending them to labour camps. They then resettled the land with German people. The Nazis planned to have as many Germans as possible inside the newly-conquered Poland.

Tata believed that his family was safest as far west and away from the Russians as possible. Since he was a tool and die maker, he was valuable to the Germans and readily accepted into the Reich (empire) as a worker.

"You are *auslanders* (foreigners)," some people said, because only Tata could speak broken German, and the rest of the family didn't know the language very well at all.

Although Halinka didn't want to be recognized as German, she wished they would call them *volkdeutsche* instead, a word referring to people of German ancestry living outside Germany. At least then they wouldn't be ostracized by some pure-bred Germans.

One day as she thought about this, she asked Mama, "How important is it to keep quiet about our Polish background?"

"Halinka, here we want people to know about our German ancestry, because that will help keep us alive. The less people know about us, the better. Remember what Tata said about watching what we say? We may meet a lot of nice people, but we don't know who to trust."

The area of Gieboldenhausen (Golden House) was still free from the direct impact of war. They didn't see any tanks or airplanes there, but they feared what might come. Field labourers, including Mama, Anne, and Therese, had to work long days without wages. Their only compensation was food and lodging.

Things were different outside of Germany, where Europe was being torn up by Hitler's war effort. Many countries were now under his tyranny, and he had his sights set on the other side of the English Channel. He was now launching massive air raids on England's military bases.

One evening just after the fall harvest was completed and the evening meal eaten, Mama, Halinka, Helen, and Paul gathered together in their room.

"Mama," Halinka moaned, "I miss Tata and Jean. Will we ever see them again?" Her eyes brimmed with tears. It had now been many weeks since they had last seen them.

"I miss them too," Mama sighed. "Every day I pray for their safety." At that moment, they were startled by a loud knock at the door.

"Come in," said Mama. The door flew open and a female officer entered.

"*Frau* Kutsche, you and your family are to relocate tomorrow morning. Be ready with your belongings by 6:00 a.m. Come with me now to receive further details."

"I will be back as soon as possible," Mama whispered. "Please look after Helen and Paul." She quickly followed the officer out the door.

At that moment, Anne and Therese entered the room. "Where is Mama being taken?" they asked.

"To see someone about us moving again," replied Halinka. "They want us ready by six o'clock tomorrow morning."

They stood silently and wondered what changes this would bring to the family.

"I hope they don't take Mama too," cried Therese.

"Girls, you must calm down and not think about such things," stated Anne firmly. "Mama will be back soon. Let's get busy and pack up our things."

"Children," Mama announced excitedly as she burst through the door, "I have lots to tell you! They're sending us to a place called Kalefeld." Her face lit up. "And the best news they told me is that Tata is alive, and we will be with him again!"

The girls squealed with joy. They could hardly believe what they were hearing.

"It's a miracle," Halinka exclaimed, her face glowing.

That night, everyone was so excited, they could barely sleep.

"Mama, was there any mention of Jean?" asked Anne as she lay in bed.

"No," replied Mama sadly. Anne's heart sank with disappointment. "But," Mama continued, "we must keep praying and believe that she is well. Now, let's try to get some sleep. Morning will come soon enough."

Halinka's mind was filled with thoughts and memories of Tata and Jean. Eventually she drifted off, but soon she felt Mama's familiar hand shaking her awake. Before long, everyone was ready and waiting for what would come next.

A knock sounded at the door. It was time to go.

Unexpected News

As they stepped outside, they were met by a cold, brisk wind. They huddled together as they were led to the truck that would take them to Kalefeld.

Kilometre after kilometre the truck rolled along narrow country roads, passing dark patches of dense forests and open, barren farm land. The reality of war was evident as they passed occasional convoys of army trucks and soldiers. Soon they found themselves surrounded by gently rolling hills.

"Look!" Halinka shouted, pointing to a sign that read Kalefeld. "We're here!"

The truck rumbled down ancient cobblestone streets. On either side were neat rows of shops and houses. They took special notice of the bakery, butcher shop, and, farther along, the church.

The truck came to an abrupt halt, and then the tailgate was opened and a guard indicated for everyone to follow him. He led them to a long, white two-and-a-half-storey stucco building divided into ten units. The guard stopped at the last unit and handed Mama a key.

"This is your new residence," he said. "You will need to go to the town office on the main street to get food ration cards from the *Burgermeister* (chairman of the town council). Heil Hitler!" He stuck his arm out straight in the Nazi salute.

Mama smiled, raised her arm, and echoed, "Heil Hitler."

Satisfied, the guard clicked his heels together, turned, and walked away. Halinka knew how much Mama did not like to salute Hitler, but it was something she had to do.

They passed through the front entrance and into a foyer. There they noticed a staircase on the left ascending to the second floor, and a door straight ahead leading to their unit. Mama unlocked the door and led them into a small main room. Through a door on the right was a kitchen with a wood stove used for both heating and cooking, a table with a bench for three people, a shelving unit, and two pails for fetching water. Other than the lone window, only a single light bulb hanging from the centre of the ceiling provided light. Straight ahead was a bedroom barely large enough for its three single beds. Adjoining this was yet another small room with one single bed.

"Put your things in here." Mama pointed to the small room. "Watch Paul and Helen while Anne and I go get our ration cards."

"Okay, Mama," answered the girls as Mama and Anne went out the door.

Paul, now over a year old, began to whine, indicating he was tired.

"Let's lay you down," Halinka said softly as she carried him to one of the beds. Therese followed and covered him with a blanket. It wasn't long before he was sound asleep.

"Let's do some exploring by looking out the kitchen window," suggested Therese, taking Helen by the hand.

"Oh my, look at all the snow!" exclaimed Halinka.

It was coming down so heavy, they could only see a short distance. Off to the right they saw the vague outline of a rectangular building. It reminded them of Tata's tool and die shop back in Poland.

"I wonder what's inside?" mused Halinka. "I sure would like to find out." She smiled and Therese nodded in agreement.

While Paul slept, the girls kept Helen occupied by telling many short stories, all of which had happy endings! The stories stood in stark contrast to their present reality of torn and tattered clothes, worn out and ill-fitting shoes, and meagre diet. Fantasies of princesses, queens, kings, and royal banquets in magnificent castles provided a well-needed distraction.

Soon Mama and Anne returned carrying a sack of food.

"Come and see what we have," called Anne. As eager eyes watched, Mama opened the sack on the table and pulled out half a dozen potatoes, one loaf of bread, a dozen eggs, margarine, matches, and two cans of evaporated milk. Although Mama realized how hungry everyone was, she knew that chores had to be completed in order to make the meal.

"Halinka, please find the water pump and bring a pail of water. Therese, locate some wood and coal for the stove. We are unit #10. Anne, when Halinka returns, you and I will wash the table. In the meantime, we can peel a few potatoes." Looking at Halinka and Therese, Mama cautioned them. "Bundle up. It's snowing hard out there."

The girls could hardly wait to explore their new surroundings.

Chapter Twenty-Four
TATA'S RETURN

As they stepped outside, Therese and Halinka were greeted by swirling, blowing snow. The ground was already covered with a thick, puffy, white blanket.

"Let's find out what's in that shed!" exclaimed Halinka as they trudged toward the building.

"Which door should we open first?" asked Therese, noticing there were three.

"You pick," laughed Halinka.

"Okay, let's try the farthest on the left."

Therese lifted the latch and swung the door open. Inside were ten small, numbered piles of neatly stacked wood and as many pails of coal. The wood would be used for cooking, and the coal was for keeping warm at night.

"Great," said Halinka, "we know where to get the wood and coal!"

"Yes," agreed Therese. "You open the next door. I'll get these after we see what's behind the other two."

They quickly made their way to the second door and discovered that it led to a large laundry tub with a hand pump for water. This was where they would wash their clothes.

"We have one more door to go. Therese, it's your turn again."

She opened it and found an outhouse—a small room with a wooden box and a seat over a dark hole.

"Okay, Therese, let's get everything Mama asked for. It's getting colder."

Their tattered shoes were no match for the deepening snow.

Therese grabbed a small pail of coal and an armful of wood while Halinka pumped water into her pail. Once loaded up, the girls plodded back through the snow. As they neared the doorway, Therese came to a sudden halt when Halinka shouted, "Wait!"

Against the stark white snow, a hint of green had caught her attention. She put her pail down and ran to a spot under the kitchen window. After scooping away some snow, she discovered a collapsed Brussels sprout plant covered with buds that resembled small cabbage heads.

"Look," she gasped.

Therese peered over her shoulder. "Let's tell Mama. Perhaps they're still good to eat. C'mon, my arms are getting tired."

Tata's Return

When they stumbled into the kitchen where Mama was busy making dinner, Halinka told her excitedly about the Brussels sprouts they had uncovered.

"Brussels sprouts?" Mama was surprised.

"Yes, right under the front window."

Grabbing her coat, Mama hurried outside and soon returned with over a dozen green sprouts. "I'm so glad you found these! You've made our meal extra special."

They spent the rest of the afternoon cleaning, preparing the meal, and keeping the fire going.

"Mama, when are we going to see Tata?" Halinka asked as she readied the table for dinner.

"Will it be today, tomorrow, or anytime soon?" asked Anne.

"I have received no information," Mama replied, "but I hope it will be soon."

After they closed the outdoor shutters for the nightly blackout, everyone gathered around the kitchen table, and the food was served.

"I'm so glad we have a place of our own," Halinka sighed. "It feels more like a real home."

Before anyone could comment, they heard a sharp rap at the door. Halinka reached for Therese's hand. *Could it be?*

Mama hurried to open the door, and a snow-covered Tata stepped inside.

"Ludwig!" Mama screamed, rushing into his open arms.

Time seemed to stand still as they all watched Mama and Tata embrace and kiss. They were so happy to see each other. Then everyone ran over to join them.

Clinging tightly to Tata, Halinka cried tears of both delight and great relief. How she had missed him! The fear of never seeing him again vanished. They were almost a whole family again. Although Jean was still missing, Halinka would never give up praying for her return.

They led Tata to the table, and after a prayer of thanksgiving, they enjoyed a good meal of potatoes, Brussels sprouts, bread, and margarine. Halinka felt like she was at a banquet in one of her make-believe stories. When the meal was completed, the girls began peppering Tata with questions.

"Where do you work, Tata?" Halinka asked.

"What do you do there?" inquired Therese.

"How did you come to be with us again?" asked Anne.

"Whoa," chuckled Tata, "let me answer one question at a time." He paused in thought before continuing. "When you saw me leave from Gieboldenhausen that day, they were taking us to a small village called Echte. They put us to work in an ore mine. My job was to maintain and repair the elevators that transported the workers in and out of the mine, and the elevators used for bringing up the ore. I also made small metal containers with lids for the *steigers* (ore mine overseers) to take to their wives, which gave me favour with them. I kept asking to be reunited with my family. After a time, my request was granted, and you have been brought to Kalefeld!"

"How far away is the mine from here, Tata?" asked Therese.

"It is within walking distance; only a few kilometres."

"What do they do with the ore?" asked Halinka.

"It is sent away to other factories where they make ammunition, such as bullets for guns and large cartridges for tanks and cannons." He lowered his voice to a hush. "There have been a lot of breakdowns in the mine. Some of the foreign workers secretly sabotage the equipment to slow production. It's the only way we can all fight back, and I am happy about it! Now remember, not a word about this to anyone ... not even amongst yourselves."

The family often passed time in the evenings listening to Tata's stories about what was happening at the mine and in the area. Halinka loved hearing them. Some stories were not so nice, like the one about the lady who had recently given some bread to a starving

Jewish woman on the street. A German soldier saw what happened and rushed over, grabbed the bread, and screamed at the woman who had given it to her.

"You do that again, and I will see that you are taken to a prison camp!" he threatened.

"Tata, I hate the Germans," interrupted Halinka. The whole family froze and stared at her, startled.

"Hush, Halinka," Tata said. "I understand how you feel. What right does one man have to tell another man that they are of lesser value than anyone else? We are all made in the image of God. God is love, and there seems to be no evidence of His love among the Nazis. It was very hard for me to remain quiet when I saw what happened to the Jewish woman. Right now, we are powerless to speak out, but many people, even some Germans, are secretly working to change things. Pray we will all succeed."

"Now," Mama interjected, "Tata and I have some other news. We've been informed that you are all required to attend school, beginning this coming Monday. Learning the German language is of the utmost importance, because it will help you to fit in."

"It's important that you are never perceived to be an enemy of Germany," Tata added. "Never give anyone a reason to accuse you of this."

The Nazis had replaced general education with teaching that would promote loyalty to Germany and

Adolf Hitler. The Kutsche children would soon find themselves confronted with this new way of thinking.

Chapter Twenty-Five
A NEW SCHOOL

Early Monday morning, the girls nervously made their way down the street. As they walked, they saw other boys and girls in school uniforms heading in the same direction. After passing through some of the downtown area, they rounded a corner, and the school came into view. It was a white, stuccoed, U-shaped building with a large clock mounted on a chimney on the peak of the roof. Eight wide steps led up to the main entrance doors.

Everywhere they went in the schoolyard, they heard children speaking German. Since it was their first day, and being very self-conscious, Halinka felt like everyone was talking about them. All she wanted to do was run and hide.

Just then, a girl with neatly braided, chestnut brown hair walked up to the girls. "*Guten morgen* (Good morning)," she smiled, extending her hand to shake theirs.

"*Guten ... morgen*," stammered Halinka.

A New School

"*Guten morgen,*" added Anne and Therese.

"My name is Hilda," continued the girl.

Before the girls could respond, a group of nearby boys began snickering, pointing, and yelling. "*Polieren! Polieren!* (Polish! Polish!)"

More snickers followed as others joined in.

Why do Germans think they are better than everyone else? Halinka thought with disgust as her hatred for Germans resurfaced once again.

"Leave them alone!" shouted Hilda, with her hands on her hips.

"Yes, leave them alone!" another boy yelled as he drew near. The unruly group grew quiet and then, one by one, walked away. Turning to the girls, he introduced himself. "My name is Wilhelm. It's nice to meet you!"

Halinka couldn't believe what had just happened. *Why are they standing up for us? Why are they being so nice to us?* At that moment, a bell rang loudly, interrupting her thoughts. Everyone lined up to enter the school.

Once inside, the girls were placed in their designated classrooms. Halinka watched as her sisters disappeared from sight. She had just found an empty desk when the teacher walked through the door and proceeded to the front of the class. Facing the students, she motioned for everyone to stand. Raising her right arm in salute, she shouted, "Heil Hitler!"

Immediately, the children responded by extending their arms and repeating "Heil Hitler" in unison. Halinka, caught off guard, gasped in surprise and threw up her arm to join in. She was too late. Her delayed response drew stares from everyone in the room. As she flushed with embarrassment, the teacher looked at her and exclaimed with a hint of amusement, "Next time, pay attention and be more prompt." Turning to address the whole class, she again raised her voice. "To the Fuhrer, a triple victory!"

"Heil! Heil! Heil!" the students responded. A wave of fear shot through Halinka as she repeated the chant and stared at the stern portrait of Adolph Hitler posted above the blackboard.

Next, the class began to sing a patriotic song. Not knowing the language or the tune, Halinka struggled to keep up. She was strangely relieved that she didn't know the words or their meaning. The song was called "Horst Wassel Lied," and it eventually became a Nazi national anthem. If she had understood, she would have found herself singing these words:

> Raise high the flag,
> The ranks are closed in tight.
> Storm Troopers march
> With firm and steady step.
> Souls of the comrades

A New School

Shot by Reds and counter might
Are in our ranks
And march along in step.
Open the road
For these, the brown battalions.
Let's clear the way
For the Storm Trooper man.
In hope, to the swastika,
Rise the eyes of millions.
Dawn breaks for freedom,
And bread for all men.
This is the final
Bugle call to arms.
Already we are set,
Prepare to fight.
Soon Hitler's flags will wave,
O'er every single street.
Enslavement ends
When soon we set things right.

They spent the rest of the day doing book work and participating in physical training. Eventually, the bell rang to signal the end of the school day.

As the girls crossed the schoolyard, they spotted Hilda and Wilhelm waving at them.

"*Auf Wiedersehen* (Goodbye)," they shouted.

The girls smiled and waved back.

"They seem very nice," said Anne.

"Yes," agreed Therese.

Halinka wished more Germans were like Hilda and Wilhelm.

"I sure didn't like the picture of Hitler in our classroom," muttered Halinka quietly as they turned onto their street.

"It made me shudder inside when we had to salute him," responded Anne.

"I couldn't even say 'Heil Hitler.' I only pretended to," confessed Therese.

As the school days progressed, the girls worked hard to learn their new language. Even though they were being taught to follow the Nazi ways, their hearts remained true to their Polish roots. Fear of what could happen to them kept them in a world of pretend. Soon, however, they would be challenged even more to keep their true feelings hidden.

Chapter Twenty-Six
HITLER YOUTH/LEAGUE OF GERMAN GIRLS

"You must join the Hitler Youth," Tata announced to Anne, Therese, and Halinka.[24]

"But Tata," protested Halinka, "how can we? We don't want to learn how to be Nazis! Our textbooks already teach us that we must love Hitler."

"We have no choice," Tata said sadly. He knew that it was a legal obligation, mandated by the Nazis. If parents objected, they would be investigated by the authorities. Students who didn't join the movement were to write an essay in which they answered the question: "Why Am I Not in the Hitler Youth?" School diplomas

---

24 The Hitler Youth movement began in the early 1920s and continued to grow as the Nazi Party increased in strength. Once Hitler came to power, all other youth movements were banned. His purpose was to indoctrinate all youth to be unquestionably loyal to the Fatherland, Germany. Hitler and the Nazis wanted the youth to believe that the Nazi Party was the only means to make Germany great. In 1933, there were 50,000 members of the youth movement, and by 1936, the membership had increased to 5.4 million. In 1939, it became mandatory for all youth to join.

could be withheld and apprenticeship opportunities turned down for those who did not join.

"You'll have your first meeting this Sunday morning at the school. I have your uniforms."

Donning their Hitler Youth uniforms that Sunday morning, the girls made their way to the school.

"I sure don't like this," whispered Halinka.

"What else can we do?" asked Anne.

"Tata said we must do this," Therese reminded them, "in order to stay safe."

"Hush," said Anne, "we're near the school."

At the school, the girls were separated by their ages to become members of the League of German Girls. Anne went with those aged fourteen to eighteen, while Halinka and Therese took a seat among the ten to thirteen-year-olds.

Every meeting opened with the German national anthem, "Horst Wassel" ("The Flag on High"), and continued for a time with the singing of other patriotic songs.

The leaders made the meetings lots of fun. The activities included storytelling, sports, hiking, camping and campfires, and marching through the village. Throughout it all was an emphasis on developing the girls to become good wives, mothers, and homemakers who would be loyal followers of the Third Reich at all costs.

Wilhelm and the boys in the Hitler Youth had a different experience. Although they took part in some similar activities, they were being prepared to be future soldiers. Much of what they did involved military-type training, such as marching, shooting, boxing, wrestling, and completing obstacle courses. The objective was to make them physically fit and obedient.

"Aren't the meetings great?" asked Wilhelm one Sunday.

"Yes," stammered Halinka, trying to express some enthusiasm.

"We just did some archery and target shooting," he continued. "I did the best at target shooting! I can hardly wait for the next practice!"

Halinka worried about Wilhelm. He was such a kind-hearted boy. He often stood up for her and Therese when others jeered at them and shouted, "*Polieren! Polieren!*" Other times he shared food with them from his family's garden. He often made them laugh with his funny jokes.

When Halinka thought of Wilhelm, she didn't think "German." He was just another human being, like her. Once, he even confided to her that he wished Hitler had never started the war. He also doubted that Germans were the superior race. She didn't want him to become a fanatical Nazi follower, someone who didn't value other human beings. Tata's words once again came to mind: "What right does one person have to tell another that they are of lesser value, for we are all made in the image of God. There are good and bad in every race. Pray we remain true to God and always do what's right." Halinka prayed this for Wilhelm often.

Over time, Wilhelm excelled at target shooting, and he won many awards. He was very proud of them and often shared his excitement with the girls. But unknown to him, his victories would prove to be costly.

Chapter Twenty-Seven
ALLIES BECOME ENEMIES

"Germany has invaded Russia!" Tata exclaimed as he returned from work one day. "They've been fighting together for almost two years to take over Europe, and now they're fighting against each other."

In June of 1941, Germany betrayed their Russian allies and launched a full-scale invasion of their country. This meant that countries that had been Russia's enemies, such as England and its allies, were now partners with them against Hitler and the Nazis. Stalin, the Russian leader, looked to both England and the United States for help, but the Americans were still neutral and not involved in the fighting. They would help by supplying weapons and raw materials, such as fuel.

"What do you think will happen now?" Mama asked, a look of worry etched on her face.

"Hopefully, all the countries fighting against Hitler will bring the war to an end sooner," answered Tata.

"Then my prayers will be answered!" Mama exclaimed tearfully.

In the weeks following the shift in the war, they noticed more troop movement throughout the area. Mama and Tata constantly warned the children to be extra careful and avoid any contact with soldiers, especially with SS personnel. As Hitler's most fierce and devoted troops, they wore distinct uniforms decorated with swastika arm bands and lightning bolt emblems, with the image of a skull on their caps. They were greatly feared by all the villagers and were known to kill people just for fun, like bullies with guns. So far, Halinka and Therese hadn't had any close encounters with them.

"Mama, I just saw a long line of soldiers walking down the main street, guarded by German troops," exclaimed Anne one day when she returned from the bakery. "There were hundreds of them, and people were whispering, 'Russian, Russian.' They looked awful!"

"Oh dear," Mama gasped.

"I'll be back," said Tata as he quickly grabbed his jacket and bolted out the front door.

Halinka and Therese looked at each other.

"Let's go see," Halinka whispered.

The girls crept quietly outside and walked briskly to the main street, where they were confronted with a terrible sight. Filling the street was a seemingly endless procession of captured Russian prisoners of war. Many were barefoot. Others were wounded and struggled to keep up. Their clothes were torn and dirty.

Many clung to each other for support, too hurt or weak to walk on their own. It was obvious that they were being forced to march a long way. The look of pain, sadness, and hopelessness on their faces horrified Halinka. There was nothing good about war!

Suddenly, Halinka saw movement out of the corner of her eye. A prisoner had just fallen. She watched as Tata rushed toward him and began to pick him up.

"Look, Therese," Halinka gasped, pointing in the direction of Tata and the fallen man.

They watched, stunned, as a German SS guard approached the men and slammed the butt of his rifle into the back of Tata's shoulder, causing him to fall over.

"Next time you will be shot!" roared the soldier.

Tata slowly got up and staggered away.

"Tata!" shrieked Halinka. She froze, suddenly realizing that the SS guard had heard her. He turned and stared directly at her with a cold, piercing look. A wave of fear rushed over her.

"Let's get out of here," Halinka whispered frantically. She grasped Therese's arm as they moved quickly through the gathering crowd of spectators and bolted away.

When they reached home, they couldn't find Tata. The girls were worried.

"Mama, have you seen Tata?" asked Halinka.

"No, I haven't," Mama replied.

"Oh no! Has Tata been taken and beaten by the SS?" Therese whispered in Halinka's ear.

Just then, the door opened and Tata walked in; he was clutching his shoulder and grimacing in pain.

"Ludwig, what's the matter?" cried Mama, rushing to his side.

"I tried to help a fallen prisoner on the street. An SS guard hit me hard with the butt of his gun."

"Let me help you," said Mama.

After removing his shirt, she applied a poultice to his wound.

Later that evening, they found out that the prisoners had spent hours moving through the village. There had been thousands of them. Those that lagged behind had been placed under guard in a barn on the edge of the village for the night. They would be forced to move on in the morning.

Up until now, there had only been occasional signs of the fighting that raged in the unseen distance. That day's experience changed everything. Lying awake in bed that evening, Halinka couldn't get the despairing faces of the prisoners out of her mind. The harsher reality of war had now arrived in Kalefeld, and unknown to her, there was still a lot more to come.

Chapter Twenty-Eight
GOOD NEWS FOR JEAN

Jean had just finished writing another letter to her family. Although she often felt homesick, it comforted her to know that she was keeping in touch with them. It was now letter number twenty-four, and she had yet to hear back from them.

Why haven't they written back? For all I know, they could be dead! She quickly pushed the thought aside.

"*Fraulein*, are you finished?" asked the matron of the hospital where Jean had been working for the past six months.

"Yes, I am," replied Jean, folding the letter and placing it in the matron's hand. "When will it be sent?"

"I will be sure to mail it right away," she responded.

The matron turned briskly away.

Unknown to Jean, her letter was placed in a container filled with many others. Although the letters were never sent, she and the other girls were encouraged to write to their families so that they would feel a connection to them and not be distracted from their many duties. The letters were examined by staff regularly for "security" reasons.

Jean had been placed in a hospital that provided short-term care for malnourished German children. By that point in the war, malnutrition wasn't very common in Germany. As the war progressed, however, it would become rampant.

Surrounded by beautiful mountains, Jean often wondered if she was in Austria. There was really no way to know where she was, as it was never spoken of. Her train trip was the longest she'd ever taken, and it took many hours.

Jean worked long hours in the kitchen, doing such things as preparing food, washing and drying dishes, and keeping it clean and orderly. She found the staff to be helpful and kind. Although hospital uniforms were required while on duty, dresses were given to them to wear when not working. On a rare day off, they loved to visit the village shops in the valley below, even though they had no money to spend.

Nazi flags and posters hung everywhere in the village. It was certainly a place that embraced Hitler.

"I'll wait out here," said Jean as her friends went into the bakery shop one day. She was in no mood to look at anything.

"May I see your papers?" asked a Nazi soldier who had quietly approached her from behind.

She nervously reached into her bag and held them out for him to see, careful to not look directly at him.

"You must be Aryan, with your blonde hair and blue eyes," he smiled. "And you work at the hospital. It is good that you are working for the Fatherland."

Jean didn't know what to say. She nodded agreeably while inwardly trembling with fright as he handed back her papers and walked away.

I look Aryan? Thank goodness he doesn't know I'm Polish.

Rumours were circulating about Germans kidnapping blonde-haired, blue-eyed young children from occupied countries and placing them in families to be raised as German citizens. The thought of Paul or little Helen being taken away from her parents, never to be seen again, was unbearable. *But what about me? Will I ever see them again?* For a moment Jean felt alone and lost in a big world that seemed to have gone mad.

"We had better get back to the hospital," stated Frieda as she came out of the bakery. This distracted Jean from her troubling thoughts. It was going to be a long, uphill walk.

Later, as the girls entered the hospital, a staff member pulled Jean aside.

"The Matron wants to see you right away."

Jean bid her friends goodbye and walked briskly to a nearby office and knocked on the door.

"Come in," responded the Matron. Noticing it was Jean, she added, "I have some good news for you. Please sit down." She waited until Jean was seated and then continued. "Your time here has come to an end. We are sending you back to your family."

The words "sending you back to your family" resounded in Jeans head.

Is this for real?

"Are you all right, Jean?" asked the Matron.

"Yes. Yes. Oh, thank you for such good news! When may I leave?"

"In three days. All the paperwork and transportation arrangements will be ready by then. Be sure you pack up. You may go now."

Jean was so excited, she could barely keep herself from running down the hall to tell her friends.

The following three days couldn't pass fast enough. Finally, the day arrived. After a tearful farewell to her friends, Jean climbed up into an awaiting train. As she found a seat and sat down, her mind filled with thoughts of being with her family again.

Will they be expecting me? Will Tata be there? Is everyone safe and still alive? The answers would come, but only after another long train ride.

Good News for Jean

Everybody stood on the station platform, anxiously awaiting Jean's arrival. Tata had insisted that all the family come, much to everyone's delight. Two days earlier, they had received word of Jean's homecoming. To Halinka, it was like a dream come true ... the family together at last!

Soon they could hear the train in the distance. Its whistle shrieked as it neared the station.

"Here it comes!" yelled Anne, jumping with excitement. Being close in age to Jean, she had especially missed her sister.

The family was temporarily enveloped in a cloud of steam as the huge engine slowly passed by and then came to a halt. The coach doors were flung open, and passengers began to disembark.

"There she is!" screamed Mama, bolting in the direction of the coming crowd. "Jean! Jean!" It seemed she couldn't get to her fast enough. How she longed to hold her daughter again.

"Mama!" sobbed Jean, throwing herself into Mama's open arms. It felt so good to be with the family at last.

Chapter Twenty-Nine
TURNING POINT

As the war progressed, Germany relied more heavily on forced labour to work in factories and on farms. By the war's end, the Nazis would have abducted about twelve million people from twenty European countries, half of which were Russians. By late autumn of 1941, many villages were overcrowded, including Kalefeld.

"Children, we must move," Mama announced after school one day. They had been in their current residence for about a year.

"But Mama, what about the garden?" asked Jean.

"We'll pick whatever we can before moving and leave the rest for whoever lives here next."

Mama certainly had a green thumb. Everything she planted in the four feet by six feet plot grew and multiplied: onions, Brussels sprouts, leeks, dill, parsley, potatoes, and pole beans. Somehow, Mama always managed to keep the family fed.

"Why?" asked Therese.

"So many other foreigners, mainly Russians, are here now," Mama continued, "and they need places to stay. Kalefeld is overcrowded."

Halinka had noticed many foreigners wearing the letter "O" on their clothing, which stood for "*Oest*" ("East"). This identified them as Eastern Europeans.

Within a week, the Kutsche family had moved to a detached home just down the street. The house had a kitchen, living room, two bedrooms, a loft above, and a cellar below. Just off the main entrance was a tiny washroom with an indoor toilet. Water had to be hand pumped. A basin used for washing both themselves and clothing was embedded in a concrete table with an opening underneath for building a fire to heat the water.

Mama was especially happy, because she'd be able to plant an even bigger garden in the larger back yard. Little did she know it would become a much greater necessity as time went on.

Halinka, Therese, and Helen were given the attic for their sleeping quarters. It was an unfinished room with rough-hewn wooden rafters. They slept on homemade beds made of hay tied together with rope and covered with sheets.

"I like our new home," Halinka whispered to Therese while they lay in bed one evening.

"Me too," Therese agreed. "We have more room, and it's fun sleeping up here!"

"I like sleeping here with both of you," Helen added, excited to be spending so much time with her older sisters.

"We like having you with us," said Therese. The girls giggled, gave each other a hug, and soon drifted off to sleep.

Although that night of December 7, 1941 was peaceful enough in Kalefeld, something else was about to happen on the other side of the world that would have a dramatic affect on all of Germany.

Hitler did everything possible to keep the German people ill-informed about the war's progress. In spite of his censorship, real news travelled secretly and swiftly amongst the people. The next day, Tata brought some amazing news when he returned from work.

"Japan has just launched a surprise air attack on the American naval base at Pearl Harbour, Hawaii. Because Japan is Germany's ally, the United States has also declared war on Germany."

"Will this bring an end to this awful war?" Mama asked, a glimmer of hope in her eyes.

"I fear that there will be a lot more trouble coming to us, but hopefully it will mean a quicker end."

Mama clasped her hands together and nodded in agreement.

The Americans had joined the allies, so Germany declared war on America. This gave Hitler a reason to attack the American ships that had been supplying his opponents with fuel, weapons, and other supplies. He was now forced to stretch his military resources even further. By this time, Germany had lost a quarter of all its troops and thousands of tanks and planes. The age of conscription in 1939 was eighteen, but now, to make up for these losses, more and more younger men were needed for active duty.

Tata did not want to alarm his family about what all this could mean. He knew that with such a large and powerful nation now involved, it was only a matter of time before there would be more widespread bombing and fighting inside Germany. Ever so steadily the cruel dangers of war marched closer toward them.

Chapter Thirty
A SECRET TOLD

Christmas 1941 in Nazi Germany had arrived. Hitler and his party were opposed to the Christian origin of Christmas, but because the German people loved the holiday so much, they couldn't do away with it. Instead, they made some changes. The name was changed to "*Rauhnacht*" (meaning the "Rough Night"). They also altered the lyrics of some songs. Any mention of the Saviour Jesus was replaced with Saviour Fuhrer (Saviour Hitler). Santa Claus became the pagan god Odin, who gave gifts. The star on top of the tree, representing the one that led the wise men to Christ, was replaced with a swastika or lightning-shaped SS symbol. Decorations became more war-like. It wasn't uncommon to hang replicas of hand grenades or machine guns on the tree. Peace on Earth because of Jesus's birth was twisted to mean that peace would only come when Germany conquered its enemies. It became a patriotic, rather than religious, celebration.

Fortunately for the Kutsche family, the small village of Kalefeld was isolated from most of this. They stayed true to their Christmas traditions and even went to a church service.

"Halinka! Merry Christmas!" It was Hilda, running toward Halinka after the service. They warmly embraced and then held each other at arm's length.

"Boy, I sure miss you!" exclaimed Halinka.

"And I miss you!" Hilda smiled warmly.

The girls had remained close friends, even though Hilda now attended a private school. It had been a few weeks since they'd last been together.

"Can you meet me tomorrow afternoon?" asked Hilda.

"I'd love to," replied Halinka. "Come with me and we'll ask Mama." They ran off to find her.

Mama turned at the sound of the approaching girls. Noticing Hilda, she smiled and said, "Hello, Hilda. It's nice to see you again! How are you?"

"I'm fine, thank you, *Frau* Kutsche. Would it be all right for Halinka to come to my place tomorrow at two o'clock?"

"Of course. I'm sure Halinka would love to visit."

Mama noticed how Halinka's face beamed with excitement.

Hilda's family owned two large textile factories, and they were very wealthy. Halinka had never been past the large gates at the entrance to their villa, so she couldn't wait to see what was inside.

The air was crisp and cold as Halinka walked along the street the following afternoon. She wrapped her shabby, worn out coat tightly around herself to stay warm. The light, powdery snow wafted away from her feet with each step.

Approaching the gate, she saw Hilda already waiting for her.

"I'm so glad you're here. Come, let's go inside." She turned toward a nearby security guard. "Could you please open the gate, Hans?" she asked.

The gate opened, and the girls made their way into the main court area.

"What a beautiful yard!" exclaimed Halinka, noticing the circular driveway and well-trimmed trees and shrubs throughout the now dormant garden. She imagined how lovely it would look when they were filled with leaves and blooming flowers.

They walked up a set of broad steps, and Hilda opened the large entrance door. Stepping inside the main foyer, Halinka could only stop and stare. It was a magnificent room with high ceilings and shiny floors. An enormous, glistening chandelier hung from the middle of the ceiling. Directly ahead of them, an elaborate, heavy wooden staircase wound its way up to the second floor.

A Secret Told

They spent the afternoon talking and enjoying cups of brause (soda pop).

"Wait here, Halinka. My mom and I have put something together for you." She disappeared around a corner and immediately returned with a large, cloth bag. "This is for you," she stated as she placed it on the floor in front of Halinka.

"What is this?" asked Halinka.

"See for yourself. Open it!"

Halinka reached in and gasped as she pulled out a beautiful, red and white checkered skirt with a lovely matching white sweater. The bag also contained two blouses, two dresses, and a navy-blue woolen coat. Hilda had outgrown all of these, and to Halinka they were a real treasure.

They couldn't buy clothing anywhere, so everything was used and reused. Until now, Halinka had only two outfits besides a school uniform and her tattered winter coat. She never thought it was possible during this time of war to receive anything so lovely.

Filled with emotion, she hugged Hilda tightly. "Thank you so much for sharing these beautiful clothes with me."

"Oh Halinka, Mom and I are so glad we can give these to you."

Before anything else could be said, they were interrupted by the sound of approaching voices. It was

Herr and *Frau* Fisher, Hilda's parents, entering an adjoining room.

"Dieter, I hope there will be an end to Hitler and this horrible war soon! Many of us are desperately praying for this."

"Erika, I too hope it will end soon. There is too much suffering everywhere. By the time this war ends, all the world will hate us. We are not the superior race as Hitler claims."

"There are many who feel the same way we do, Dieter, but these Nazi bullies do not give us a choice."

"I know, but we must stop this kind of talk. Should anyone hear us, we could be reported and turned over to the Gestapo."

Taking Halinka by the hand, Hilda motioned for her to pick up the bag, and then she quietly led her from the room and out the front door.

"Please don't mention what my parents said to anyone," Hilda pleaded. "We would be in serious trouble, even taken to a concentration camp, if the Nazis found out!"

"I would never tell anyone," Halinka reassured her. "I and my family are against them too."

"You had best get going so my parents don't find out you've heard them."

Once out the gate, Halinka walked quickly, clinging the bag tightly to her chest. How thankful she was to know that there were German people who opposed Hitler too. In fact, by the war's end, twenty-five attempts would be made on Hitler's life, many by his own people. Not too far from Kalefeld, a baron's only son was executed for such an attempt. Suddenly, Halinka realized that the hatred she had harboured for all Germans had melted away. They were not all bad.

Still, she had to be careful. There were some even in Kalefeld who wouldn't think twice about reporting someone to the Gestapo. Although Halinka was aware of some of the Nazi's evil, she had no idea of the awful devastation they had caused in other countries, especially toward the Jews.

Chapter Thirty-One
STRUGGLING TO ESCAPE HUNGER

"Halinka! Therese!" shouted Mama. "It's time to get more grass for the rabbits."

"Yes, Mama," replied Halinka. The girls were sitting on the makeshift swings Tata had made for them in the back yard. About every third day they would walk over a kilometre toward the ore mine and gather the tall grass growing along the sides of the road. Using sickles, they would cut the grass and fill the wagon with it. They made a point of finishing up around the time Tata would be returning from work.

"Here he comes!" Therese shouted, pointing up the hill. They waved their arms to get his attention. He waved back and continued limping closer. They could see the limp getting worse. Tata had been shot through his leg many years earlier, and it had never completely healed. Although he was in constant pain, they never heard him complain. His most dreaded fears were that he would be found unfit for work, unable to provide for his family, or worse, be sent to a concentration camp. He had already received one threat: if he didn't show up for work, he would be considered useless and sent to a camp.

"Hop on, Tata," said Halinka. They wanted to help him as much as possible, since he had to walk about six kilometres each day, to and from work.

Tata gently settled himself into the wagon. The girls laughed as they pulled him down the long slope toward home.

Once home, Tata went into the house to clean up while the girls unloaded the grass and fed the rabbits.

"I can't believe how much they eat!" exclaimed Therese. "If I ate that much, I'd be the size of a house!"

"Therese, you are as skinny as a rail," laughed Halinka. "You would have to eat a lot more than what they eat!"

They were thankful for the rabbits. They not only provided meat for the table but also bones for soup, and fur for hats and mittens. Nothing was wasted.

Early in the war, Hitler had determined that the German people would have enough to eat. He wanted them comfortable and positive about his ambitions; otherwise, they might become unhappy and turn against him. By acquiring slave labour and plundered food from other countries, he had easily supplied their needs. He also established a rationing system that used colour-coded ration cards. They were divided into different values of ten, twenty-five, fifty, one hundred, and five hundred grams for items such as coal, meat, imitation coffee, dairy, sugar, flour, and eggs.

Theft of food stamps was considered a serious crime, and offenders were sent to labour camps. Later, those convicted of using counterfeit stamps were given the death penalty.

When Germany and Russia began fighting each other, things changed. The large amount of food that came from Russia was no longer available. After the spring of 1942, the daily ration per family dropped to half. Whipped cream, cakes, table cream, and chocolate had not been available since the beginning of the war. Coffee substitutes were made from roasted barley, rye, and chicory. Vegetables grown locally were available only when in season. People became more resourceful at finding edible foods in the wild.

It wasn't uncommon for Halinka and Therese to spend hours in farmers' fields gathering grain and sugar beets left behind by the harvesters. They took the grain to the local mill and exchanged it for flour. Mama could then make bread from the flour. The sugar beets were cleaned and boiled for twelve hours into a thick syrup, which was served frequently as a spread on bread and as a sugar substitute. Many times, turnips and sugar beets were the only foods available. By the war's end, Halinka was so tired of the taste, she never wanted to eat them again. It was especially important for Mama to eat well. She was soon to have a baby!

Chapter Thirty-Two
TAKEN

Baby John was born in October of 1942, and Mama was now busier than ever. Thankfully, Jean had just returned from her one year of service and could lend a hand. It was mandatory for the older members of the "League of German Girls" to put in one year of service for the Fatherland, because the boys were sent into regular military service. Jean had spent the previous year living and working on a farm and helping with planting, weeding, harvesting, and tending livestock.

"Girls." Mama spoke to Halinka and Therese. "Please take this food stamp and get us a loaf of bread."

"Sure, Mama," Therese said as Halinka took the stamp from Mama's outstretched hand.

Later, as they were leaving the bakery, Halinka spotted Wilhelm across the street.

"Wilhelm!" shouted Halinka.

He turned, smiled, and immediately darted toward them.

"Hi, girls, it's good to see you again!" He gave them each a hug. "How's everyone doing?" His big smile always warmed their hearts.

"We're as well as can be. Jean has returned home, and baby John is now over six months old. How about yourself?"

"I'm very busy with the HJ (Hitler Youth). In fact, I think I'm as fast as a fox now!" He laughed. "And I'm still winning a lot of target shooting awards. My leaders say I'm the best! Can you believe it?" He shrugged nonchalantly.

"Aren't you worried they'll make you go to war?" Therese asked.

"No, not me. I'm only fourteen. I'm way too young." Then, in a whisper, he added, "I hope this war's over before I'm of age to fight."

Without realizing it, Wilhelm was voicing the thought of a growing number of German people. Many were saying, "Better an end with terror, than terror without end!"

The Nazi leaders were well aware of the dangers of ruling by terror. They wanted the world to believe that all German people stood united behind Hitler. In reality, it was only through terror and fear that they were able to control the increasing number of disappointed and war-weary people. They punished, threatened, and shot their own people to remain in control. More people were realizing that if Adolf Hitler had not come to power, there would not have been a war!

Germany was in a poor state and lacked the resources to fight in so many different places at the same time. At the beginning of the war, the youngest of conscripted soldiers were eighteen. As the war progressed, the age dropped lower. It wasn't uncommon for sixteen-year-old youths to be conscripted against the will of their parents. In their desperation, women, especially mothers, became more outspoken in their opposition to the war. In Berlin, a large crowd of weeping women broke through the barrier when a train arrived, filled with severely wounded soldiers.[25] In other cities, women were shouting, "Make an end to the war. We want our men back!" As the war intensified, so did the unrest inside Germany. Unfortunately, more losses and destruction would have to come before they gained freedom from Hitler's strangling grip. People were desperately praying for an end to it all.

A week later, Therese thought it would be a good idea to have Wilhelm join them to get grass for the rabbits.

---

25 Kantorowicz, 22.

"Halinka, let's see if Wilhelm will join us this morning. Hopefully he won't be busy with the HJ."

"Good idea. Let's tell Mama and get going."

About ten minutes later, the girls neared Wilhelm's front door. As they were about to knock, they heard a deep wail inside the house, which caused them to freeze. Immediately, Halinka thought of the sounds she heard from the suffering people crammed on the freight trains a few years earlier in Wolkowysk. Something was wrong here!

With their hearts racing, they knocked on the door, dreading what they might discover.

Slowly the door opened. Wilhelm's mother stood before them, her face as white as a ghost. Her eyes were bloodshot from crying.

"Wha ... what's wrong, *Frau* Ricther?" asked Halinka.

"Wilhelm ... he's gone," she stammered. "They've taken him!"

"No!" screamed the girls.

At age fourteen, Wilhelm had been conscripted to fight!

Chapter Thirty-Three
BOMBS

Since the family's arrival in Germany, it had been standard practice to black out homes and businesses by shuttering and sealing all windows before dark. Halinka and Therese had been given the responsibility of closing and latching the outside shutters. It was also common to see a van with loudspeakers instructing people to find shelter should they hear the sound of an air raid siren. People caught in a raid downtown were to use a common bomb shelter in the basement of a large church; otherwise, they would use their own cellars. Larger cities had many more public shelters.

Occasionally, planes could be heard flying overhead. Many were German, but Britain and its allies had also been sending spy planes to locate targets such as railways, factories, and military bases. Major cities had also been experiencing bombing as early as 1940. Unbeknownst to them, the nearby city of Hanover, an hour away, was about to experience its most severe

Bombs

attack. Kalefeld and the ore mine at Echte where Tata worked, had been recently designated as targets.

"Therese, do you hear that?" asked Halinka as they lay in the loft early one morning.

"Yes," she replied. "What is it?"

They strained their ears as they listened to the drone of a lone plane. "Maybe it's one of those spy planes Tata was talking about. There have been a lot more of them lately."

"I noticed that too," Halinka added. *Could they be coming to bomb here?* It was a scary thought!

On October 8, 1943, Halinka and Therese had just left Hilda's house. They'd stayed longer than intended and knew that they needed to get home to close the shutters before the nightly curfew. Hurrying down the now-deserted streets, they heard a short warning whistle.

Oh no! An attack is coming!

Gasping for breath and running as fast as they could, they knew they had to reach home before the alarm sounded. It was too late! The slow, deafening sound of the air raid siren began to blow until it reached its high pitch. After the third loud blast, when everyone should have been in a shelter, it grew quiet. Therese and Halinka were still out in the open. As they hurried for home, they heard a low droning sound off in the distance, which steadily grew louder. Soon, even the air around them and the earth beneath them seemed to vibrate from the noise. What was coming?

"Run faster!" screamed Therese. By now their bodies were shaking from the vibrations.

They looked up at the sky and were terrified at the sight—hundreds of huge airplanes as far as they could see.

"Oh God, help us!" Halinka cried, fearful that bombs would soon fall on them.

The girls ran with all their might to reach home under the thundering roar.

As they rounded the street corner, they spotted Tata standing in the doorway. When he saw them, he threw his hands in the air, thankful to see his girls.

"Inside, quickly!" he screamed, closing the door behind and following them down into the cellar, where everyone was gathered.

When Mama saw them, she jumped up and pulled them close. They huddled together on strewn hay while Tata handed them each a blanket. They had no idea how long they would have to remain there. Perhaps throughout the night?

Clinging together in the light of a single candle, they silently prayed and waited for the bombs to fall. They never did. Instead, the hundreds of RAF bombers continued on their way to Hanover, just a hundred kilometres away.

Bombs

That evening, the RAF carried out two big attacks on Hanover. A total of 504 aircraft were involved. The bombing was concentrated and accurate. It was the most devastating Allied attack on the city during the war, with over a thousand people killed and many injured. Almost four thousand buildings were destroyed, and thirty thousand were damaged. The main railway station and surrounding buildings were completely gutted from the explosive fires.

From down in the cellar, the family heard the last of the planes flying off into the distance. Soon, the earth around them began to shake.

"They're dropping bombs," whispered Tata.

Halinka shuddered, knowing that something or someone was being destroyed. How she wished this war would end.

Although the shaking continued, the danger was elsewhere, so the all-clear siren sounded.

"Come," said Tata, "we can go upstairs now."

They peeked out the door facing Hanover. The glow on the horizon looked like the sun was about to rise. The city was on fire!

It was becoming more dangerous for Kalefeld, and this was only the beginning.

Chapter Thirty-Four
TOO CLOSE!

The warning sirens and the run for shelter became a daily routine. Destruction and death were a common occurrence. By war's end, Hanover would have suffered from eighty-eight raids. So far, Kalefeld had been spared.

Suddenly, they heard the warning siren.

"Quick, everyone to the basement!" Mama ordered as the sirens blew their familiar sound.

Seconds later, huddled in the basement, they listened to the familiar drone of airplanes overhead. They knew that after the planes passed by, they would feel the faint shaking of the earth from far-off explosions.

On that day, however, before they felt any rumbles, they heard the sound of an approaching plane and then an eerie, screaming cry from the sky.

"Cover your heads!" shouted Tata with alarm in his voice. A bomb was coming their way!

With one hand over her head, and the other clasping Therese's tightly, Halinka wondered, *Is this it? Are we going to die?*

"Wheeeeeezzz!" The whistling sound of the falling bomb grew louder, lowering in pitch as it neared the ground. It was a monstrous sound! Halinka was sure it was about to land right on top of them!

With a deafening explosion, the house shook violently and creaked like it was about to collapse on top of them. Their eyes stung as they gasped for air in the dust-filled room. Again and again the bombs fell. After five earth-shattering explosions, it stopped. Coughing and choking, they anxiously waited for another, but all they could hear was the sound of the single aircraft receding into the distance.

Halinka held her breath. Would it return, or were more coming? They had no idea. For tonight ... they were alive! It was a night of terror they would never forget. With the dust drifting around them, and their ears still ringing from the noise, Tata instructed everyone to stay put for the night. What would Kalefeld look like in the morning?

Early the next morning, they cautiously climbed up and out of the basement.

"I thank God we all survived," Tata said before leaving for work. "I'm sure they were after the tracks." He knew it was important for the Allies to disrupt the movement of the German ore being shipped to make munitions.

After Tata left, the girls' curiosity got the best of them. They wanted to see where the bombs had fallen.

"Therese, let's go have a look," suggested Halinka.

They scurried outside, crossed the street, and walked over the bridge to the train tracks. Just on the other side, they saw a large crater. Halinka shuddered, realizing that it was only about one hundred metres from their home, and even closer to those on that side of the street.

"Look at that!" exclaimed Therese, pointing at the large hole.

"That must be where one of the bombs fell," said Halinka. "Come on, let's get a closer look."

"Wow, it's huge!" The girls peered over the edge.

"I'm sure our whole house could fit inside," Halinka remarked.

As they walked along the tracks, they discovered four more huge craters. Clearly the tracks had been the intended target but were missed. Would they be back to finish the job?

Chapter Thirty-Five
NORTHEIM

On April 6, 1945, Halinka and Therese walked with Anne to the train station. She was on her way to Northeim, about ten kilometres south of Kalefeld, to attend school.

"Thanks for keeping me company," smiled Anne as they reached the platform. The whistle of the incoming train shrilled loudly as it drew near. As it came to a stop, they were momentarily engulfed in a thick cloud of steam. The doors opened, the girls hugged Anne goodbye, and she climbed aboard. They waved at each other as the train slowly pulled away.

Anne had been attending the Tailor/Dressmaking School in Northeim for the past six months. She loved learning to make her own patterns and designing suits, coats, blouses, shirts, and slacks. There was a lot to learn, but she was eager.

Sitting at her sewing machine while stitching together jackets one day, the time seemed to fly by quickly. Shortly after the lunch break, in the early afternoon, everyone was abruptly startled by the sound of the air raid warning signal.

The instructor shouted, "Everyone to the shelter!"

With sirens blaring, the students streamed out the door, down the now-crowded street, and into their designated bomb shelter. Huddled in a corner of the room, Anne braced herself for what she knew would come next. Suddenly, the explosions and shaking began. It was her first time going through an air raid without her family, and she had never felt so alone and scared. Over the ear-piercing sounds of falling bombs and explosions, she could hear the screams and cries from women and children. The building quaked violently. Bomb after bomb exploded, and the uncertainty of surviving consumed her.

"Help us, Lord!" she sobbed.

Much to her relief, it ended moments later. An eerie silence permeated the room, and everyone remained motionless, waiting to see if more would come. Thankfully, the all-clear siren rang out. They were safe, but above ground there was much damage.

That day, a squadron of just under one hundred US bombers had attacked the railyards of both Gottingen (about twenty kilometres south of Northeim) and Northeim.

Reaching the street level, Anne gasped and stood in bewilderment at the sight before her. The nearby train station, the tracks, and many surrounding houses and buildings had been totally destroyed. People were running in panic everywhere.

I'm sure they were after the tracks. Anne remembered Tata's words when Kalefeld had been bombed. *Did they bomb Kalefeld today too?* She had to find out! Realizing she had no way back, and driven by desperation to find out if her family was still alive, she began running home with all her might. The thought of losing them was unbearable.

With her heart pounding wildly, and gasping for each breath, Anne pushed herself nonstop over the hilly terrain for almost two hours. She thought she would collapse from exhaustion, but nothing could stop her!

Relief washed over her as Kalefeld finally came into view and she saw no signs of destruction. Staggering down the street to the house, she flung open the door and fell onto the floor.

"Anne!" Mama screamed, rushing to her side. "You're safe! We were told Northeim was bombed!"

They wept, thankful to still be alive.

The following day, over 260 bombers struck the railyards in Northeim again, as well as two other nearby towns. Throughout Germany, massive bombing campaigns were underway. Some entire cities were destroyed in one night. Russia was advancing from the east, while Britain and its allies were coming from the west. Thousands of German soldiers were surrendering daily. Would they be able to endure to the end?

Chapter Thirty-Six
SURRENDER!

By the late spring of 1945, Germany was in disarray, and terror had increased everywhere—not just from Hitler and the Nazis, but from the skies and the knowledge that other armies were coming to invade Germany. Although they desperately wanted the war to end, they understood many lives would be lost.

People were starving. Food was so scarce, even ration cards were often of no use. Mama and the family did everything possible just to stay alive. The produce from the garden, the eggs, and the rare meal of rabbit meat barely sustained them. Sugar beet syrup and turnips! Too often throughout the past winter, that was all they had. On one occasion, Mama sent Halinka to see if bread was available at the bakery. To her relief, on that day, it was.

The aroma of the freshly baked loaf of bread wafted up from the bag as she was returning home. *Just one little taste!* It smelled too good to resist. Before she knew it, she had poked a hole with her forefinger into the end of the loaf and was carefully pulling out a bite-sized piece. Chewing it slowly, she savoured the taste as hunger compelled her to do it again and again ...

"Here's the bread, Mama." Halinka warily placed the bag on the table.

"Thank you, Halinka." Mama pulled the loaf partially out, took a nearby knife, and began to slice it. She gasped! There was a large hole in the interior.

"Halinka, how could you?" Mama asked sharply, turning toward her. Tata walked into the room and noticed the partially eaten loaf.

"Olga," he admonished, "do not be upset. It was not disobedience that caused her to do this. It was hunger."

Mama looked at Halinka, who had burst into tears, full of shame. "Tata is right," she sighed, wrapping her arms around her. "I wish I could take your hunger away."

On top of the extreme hunger, Tata's health had been steadily deteriorating. Without proper nutrition or medical help, he couldn't recover from his damaged and infected foot and leg. He was grateful that Halinka and Therese brought him part way home each day. Even so, he didn't know how much longer he could continue. Being sent to a concentration camp seemed more possible than ever. It was a race of time between how long he could hold out and when the war would end.

By this time, the majority of Germans no longer believed Hitler's propaganda. Many now said, "If Hitler said it, it's not true!" He used over 300,000 SS guards and at least another 150,000 armed police and extra forces just to control his own German people. Even the military personnel had been disillusioned for quite some time. Soldiers on the front lines were turning to drastic measures to get out of fighting. Many ate soap or chemicals to get sick and be declared unfit for duty. Others shot themselves in the arm or foot. Desertion became increasingly common.[26]

Germany's army was weakening, and the Allied Forces were advancing everywhere. It wasn't uncommon to hear the sound of gunfire in the nearby hills. Even in Kalefeld, an American tank battalion had recently passed through while carrying over a dozen captured German soldiers. At the sight of them, Halinka worried and wondered about Wilhelm. Was he safe?

After dinner one evening, just before dusk, Tata was returning from the downtown area. As he approached the bridge, he noticed a young boy wearing a German infantry uniform and standing on the edge. He was crying.

"Can I help you?" Tata asked.

---

26 Kantorowicz, 26.

"I didn't want to fight!" he sobbed. "They made me! They threatened to send my family to prison. I had no choice. Now we are retreating because the British are coming. When I get caught, they'll kill me anyway, so I might as well jump into the river and die."

Fearing he would do just that, Tata said, "No, son. Come with me."

The boy stared at him in disbelief.

"Please, you can trust me," Tata urged, moving closer. He took him gently by the arm and led him along the street, limping as quickly as he could. "We have no time to lose. The British could be here any time."

Halinka was about to go out the side door when it suddenly opened. There stood Tata and a young German soldier by his side. She gasped in surprise and stepped out of the way as they entered.

"Close the door, Halinka." Tata ordered as he led the boy into the kitchen. "Olga, please get some clothes for him."

"What's going on?" she asked.

"This boy is not a Nazi. He was forced to fight and wants out. We must protect him. First thing, we must get rid of his uniform."

"Come," Mama said, waving for him to follow.

Halinka shuddered as she thought of Wilhelm. He too had been forced to join the army. *Is he in trouble like this boy? Has he been caught, shot, or left for dead somewhere?*

Surrender!

As her eyes began to blur with tears, she pushed the unbearable thoughts aside.

"God, please protect him," she quietly prayed.

Minutes later, Mama and the boy returned. He was now wearing shorts and a shirt. Tata took the uniform, hurried to the outhouse, and tossed it down into the foul-smelling water. He pushed it under and out of sight with a long stick.

As dusk fell, everyone stood silently in the kitchen as Tata returned. It had been a close call! They could now hear the rumbling, clanking sound of tanks arriving at the outskirts of town. The noise grew louder as the heavy equipment moved closer. Was this the sound of freedom for the German people? They could only hope. Unknown to them, their part of the country was now considered the British zone, and the invading troops included Canadian soldiers.

"Halinka, Therese, grab a white sheet off your bed and hang it out the upstairs windows," Mama ordered, her voice shrill with excitement. "This is truly an answer to our prayers." She could hardly contain herself.

Hurrying up the stairs, the girls grabbed a sheet from off the hay. They tied a piece of heavy yarn to opposite corners, opened the windows, and hung it from ledge to ledge, securing the ends to the handles.

"We surrender! We surrender!" they shouted, watching in awe as tanks and other vehicles moved slowly past them on the street below. Soldiers on foot were spreading out and going from house to house to look for German soldiers. Four of them were walking toward their home. *Will they take the boy away?* Halinka wondered. They quickly made their way down the ladder to the kitchen.

Halinka was about to tell Tata about the approaching soldiers when a loud knock at the door interrupted her. They froze in fear. For six years they had lived in distress, dreading the Nazis. What would the enemies of Germany be like?

"Sit around the table and do not say a word," Tata whispered. "I will do the talking."

When he opened the door, he saw two British soldiers standing before him.

In broken German, one of them asked, "Is there anyone from the German army here?"

"Come in and see for yourselves." Tata moved aside as they entered and went from room to room, guns at the ready. When they were satisfied that no enemies were present, they departed to continue searching elsewhere.

The young boy sighed with relief and threw his arms around Tata. "Thank you. I will never forget what you have done for me! You have set me free!"

"Son, we have all been set free."

That night, everyone had trouble sleeping. They no longer feared Hitler and the Nazis but the unknown. What would their new world bring?

Chapter Thirty-Seven
FREEDOM!

Just after sunrise the next morning, Halinka and Therese were awoken by voices in the street below. They moved the shutters ever so slightly and peeked out. Tanks, trucks, and jeeps were parked everywhere. Directly across from them stood a small, green, two-wheeled trailer with a stove and chimney. It was a field kitchen!

Field kitchens, also called mobile canteens, were used to provide warm food to troops, either in temporary encampments or near the front lines close to the fighting. They were usually pulled by a supply truck.

A soldier was serving food and drinks. The whole scene seemed calm and relaxed. Some soldiers were smiling and laughing.

To their surprise, they saw Jean and Anne being offered hot, steaming drinks.

"What are they doing over there?" Halinka whispered.

"I don't know," replied Therese, "but these soldiers don't seem mean like the Nazis."

Halinka shuddered at the thought of Hitler's soldiers. She was glad they were gone.

"Let's get dressed and go down," suggested Halinka.

As they reached the bottom of the stairs, Anne and Jean rushed in through the side door, smiling and bursting with excitement.

"That was the best coffee I've ever had in my whole life!" shouted Anne.

"The soldier called it camp coffee," remarked Jean.

It had been a very long time since anyone in the family had tasted real coffee.

Camp coffee was a liquid made with real coffee and chicory extract. They prepared it by adding the concentrate to boiling water.

"Come on," said Halinka, suddenly feeling very brave, "let's go see what's happening."

She grabbed Therese by the hand and pulled her out the door. They quietly made their way to the street and were immediately spotted by a soldier. He smiled and walked toward them. They felt uncertain, not sure of what to do. As he drew closer, he pointed to himself and said, "I am a Canadian from Canada. We have come to set you free." The girls had never heard of Canada and had no idea what it meant. He smiled, reached into a pocket, and pulled out some small, flat objects wrapped in brown paper. He offered one to each of them.

"Try one of these," the soldier said. They looked quizzically at them, not knowing what to do. He laughed and removed the two wrappings from his own piece. Folding it in half, he put it in his mouth and began to chew. Using his hands, he encouraged them to do the same. Suddenly, a large bubble emerged from between his lips. The girls stared in awe. They had never seen anything like it! After unwrapping and putting the gum in their mouths, they began to chew, savouring the delicious, sweet taste of peppermint. It had been years since they'd tasted anything so good. They spent the next several minutes laughing and having fun with this uniformed stranger, learning how to chew gum and blow bubbles. His kindness and friendliness overwhelmed them. They had been in fear for so long, it was hard to believe that this was really happening. Was this truly the beginning of freedom? No more Nazis? No more SS? No more Gestapo?

A few days later, the long-awaited words arrived: "Germany has surrendered! The war in Europe is over!" At first, everyone erupted with cheering and dancing in the streets, but after the initial celebrating, another reality set in. Germany had paid a horrendous cost. The loss of lives and destruction was massive.

Food and medicine and other necessities were either in short supply or non-existent. It would take many months to recover. In the meantime, over a million civilians would die of starvation and sickness.

Many, including Tata, sought information from the Red Cross about missing relatives, but progress was slow. Most of the lines of communication had been destroyed or damaged. The Red Cross and other aid groups were overwhelmed and short of supplies.

Returning from the Red Cross depot one day, Tata brought someone home. No one recognized him.

"Children, it's your Uncle Ernest."

Halinka covered her mouth with her hand and gasped. Everyone else just stood speechless. His head was bruised and swollen, and he had a deep gash on his forehead. The old clothes he wore hung limply, as though many sizes too large, except where his stomach protruded. The once happy sparkle in his eyes was gone. He was on the verge of dying of starvation! Had the war lasted another week, he would not have survived.

"Come, Uncle Ernest, sit down." Mama gently put her arm around his shoulder and led him to the kitchen, where she fed him a small amount of mushy food.

During his slow recovery, he told them what had happened. When the Nazis banned ownership of shortwave radios, Uncle Ernest did not hand his in, even after Tata pleaded with him to give it up. A month before the war ended, on his way to have it repaired, he got caught. The Nazis arrested him as a spy and placed him in a concentration camp, where he was beaten and starved. Now, Mama was determined to make him well again.

"Halinka, Therese," asked Anne one morning, "have you heard anything about Wilhelm?"

"No," replied Halinka, shaking her head sadly. "We're still hoping he survived."

"We just can't give up," added Therese.

Many nights they had lay awake, praying for him. When they would hear that injured soldiers were coming back from the front, they would go to the train station to see if Wilhelm was among them. Often, the girls had thought they had seen him, only to discover that it was someone else. Hope of his survival was slipping away. Too many German soldiers had already been confirmed dead.

Only yesterday they had stopped in to visit his mother, *Frau* Fischer. She was quite distraught, as there was no news of him at all. Perhaps the unthinkable had happened and Wilhelm was not coming home.

Mama walked into the room, interrupting the girls' conversation.

"Halinka, please take this voucher and see if the bakery has any bread."

"I'll go too," offered Therese.

Freedom!

Early that morning, after many days without, the bakery had received a supply of flour and had made fresh loaves of bread. Therese clutched the single loaf protectively as they exited the bakery. She would not allow Halinka to be tempted to eat it as she had been one other time!

Making their way along the street, Halinka saw a lone figure off in the distance coming toward them. She noticed the person had a limp and appeared to struggle. *Another soldier, no doubt, returning home.*

Turning to cross the street, Halinka cast one more glance at the lone figure. Something about him caught her eye. With her heart pounding wildly, she grabbed her sister's hand. "Could that be Wilhelm?"

"I'm not sure," replied Therese, turning to stare at the approaching figure, "but we must find out!"

Quickening their steps, they heard a shout.

"Therese! Halinka!"

They recognized it instantly as the sweet, familiar voice of Wilhelm.

Time seemed to stand still as they raced toward him and fell into his open arms.

"You made it, Wilhelm!" Therese cried.

"Yes, and you made it too!" he replied, embracing them both tightly.

"It's a miracle!" Halinka shouted. "We made it! We endured until the end!"

In the coming weeks, more of the family was reunited. Zigmund, Auntie, Uncle Leopold ... everyone they hadn't seen for five long years.

World War II was the deadliest conflict in human history up to that point. Thirty countries, about 100,000,000 people, were directly involved, and about 80,000,000 people were either injured or died.[27]

---

27 Before the war would finally come to an end, the Nazis would kill five million Poles. The Russians would kill one million. One out of every six people in Poland would die. Every family would be affected.

WHAT HAPPENED TO...

Rex: Survived the war and lived to a ripe old age in Wolkowysk with their ex-nanny.

Irka and her parents: Unknown.

Uncle Leopold: Survived the war and remained in West Germany.

Uncle Ernest: Survived the war and lived in East Germany under communist rule.

Auntie and Cousin Zigmund: Survived the war, returned to Poland, and lived under communist rule.

Wilhelm: Was conscripted at age fourteen and forced to shoot down enemy aircraft. If he had refused, he would have been shot and killed by SS troops. At one point while retreating, he fell off an army truck, was rolled into a ditch by his fellow soldiers, and left to die. He had broken both hips. Eventually, a farmer's wife heard him moaning, found him, and took him in a wheelbarrow to a nearby makeshift hospital. He was placed in traction for six months. Later, he was sent back out to fight again until the war's end.

Hilda and her family: Survived the war and remained in Kalefeld.

Kutsche Family: Survived the war and later came to Canada, at separate times, between 1949–1960.

The young German soldier Tata brought home at war's end was reunited through the Red Cross with his family after the war.

See photos of the people who inspired this story:

www.enduringtheempire.com

AUTHOR'S NOTE

Most of the events in this story are true and based on my mother, Halinka's, recollection of life in Poland during World War II. Other information was gathered from her older siblings Jean and Anne, who were both still alive at the time of this writing. Therese passed away at the age of fifty-six in 1986. In order to better engage the reader, I have taken some artistic liberties and added a few fictional events and characters.